PURCHASE DECISION AND CONSUMER BEHAVIOUR

PURCHASE DECISION AND CONSUMER BEHAVIOUR

DR. A. VINAYAGAMOORTHY
Lecturer
Department of Commerce
Bharathiar University
Coimbatore - 641 046
Tamil Nadu

SERIALS PUBLICATIONS
NEW DELHI

First Published - 2005

ISBN : 81-86771-36-0

Published by

Head Office : **SERIALS PUBLICATIONS**
4, B.S.S. Hall, Khyber Pass Market
Civil Lines, Delhi-110054 (India)
Phone : 23245225
Fax : 91-11-23272135
E-mail: serials@satyam.net.in

Branch Office : 4830/24, Prahlad Street, Ansari Road
Darya Ganj, New Delhi-110002 (India)

Contents

Preface

Intelligent marketing commercialises a product, helps flourish an industry, develops an economy and satisfies consumer needs. Marketing is an important functional area of business management and assumes a top position in today's economy.

This book is designed in such a way that it covers the relevant syllabi of the universities in India. The book presents a comprehensive coverage of the subject with examples from the Indian scenario. The book stresses on purchase decision and consumer behaviour and clearly explains the five stages of problem recognition, information search, information sources, evaluation of alternatives and factors influencing the consumers in the decision-making process. It also explains outlet selection and purchase.

The external environment and its influence on decision-making is highlighted. These are demographical, political, cultural and technological factors. Along with these, the internal determinants of beliefs, attitudes, personality, memory and values have also been discussed in this book.

The marketing manager must know about the changing attitudes, beliefs, interests and moods of consumer and must be able to woo the consumer by changing the marketing mix. While marketing the product, the satisfaction of the consumer is of prime importance and the repeat purchase must be ensured, so that, the product is on a sound footing. All these factors have been highlighted throughout the text.

The author has taken every endeavour to incorporate new ideas and concepts in the field. He has drawn freely on various sources–textbooks, periodicals, bulletins etc.–in the preparation of this book. Sincere efforts have been taken to explain the theories in a lucid, easy and understandable language.

It is hoped that this book will serve as a useful text for students and teachers. The author will be happy to receive any feedback, which may help in improving the book in its subsequent editions.

Dr. A. Vinayagamoorthy

Acknowledgements

In Planning and completing this research project, I have drawn help from various sources and wishes to acknowledge them with a sense of gratitude and appreciation.

It is with all the sincerity at my command and from the deepest abyss of my heart, I express my thanks to those connected with the successful completion of the thesis. Among the large number of individuals, one person stands out and that is my guide **Dr. K. Padmanabhan,** Head and Professor of Economics, Sacred Heart College, (Autonomous), Tirupattur-635 601, Vellore District, Tamil Nadu. I am especially grateful to my guide for his patience with and understanding of the pressures under which a doctoral candidate often has to work. As my guide and supervisor, he provided many valuable insights on theory, subject matter and analysis. His editorial comments were always to the point and his generous and spirited guidance helped me to pull the work to final completion.

As he is a stickler for perfection with a higher sense of honesty, it was a pleasure to work under him. His critical remarks were coupled with educative comments. In my opinion, he was a guide par excellence. He was a good guide because he would sit with me and hear my point of view before accepting or rejecting it, a trait, which, I am told, very few guides possess. How lucky I was to learn not only the art of teaching but also the noble act of tolerance from him!.

Dr. S. Yuvaraj, Lecturer, Department of Commerce, University of Madras, has extended his helping hand kindly and generously to me in more ways than one in the preparation and completion of the thesis. Words fail me when

I try to thank him. He was totally responsible in the analysis of the data gathered. This knowledge of statistical analysis using the computer is phenomenal. His motto, 'Systematic Perseverance', yields right results and has worked well on a number of occasions. I doubt if I can ever repay my debt of gratitude I owe him.

I owe a deep debt of gratitude to Dr. D. Amarchand, the Registrar, (Retd.), University of Madras, and Dr. M. Ranganathan, Professor and Officiating Head of the Department of Commerce, University of Madras, for all their guidance and support.

I extend my sincere thanks to Dr. S. Sivasubramanian, Vice Chancellor, Thiru V.C. Thangavel, Registrar i/c, Bharathiar University, Coimbatore - 641 046, Dr. M. Manickam, Professor and Head, Dr. S. Sudalaimuthu, Dr. Dhanabhakyam, Dr. P. chellasamy, Lecturers, Department of Commerce, Bharathiar University, Coimbatore for their appreciation and earnest support given to me in publishing this book.

My special thanks to the Former Principal, Sacred Heart College, Tirupattur, Rev. Fr. Dr. P. P. George, SDB, who gave me permission to do Ph.D. at Sacred Heart College.

The Sacred Heart College of Tirupattur, under the guidance of Rev. Fr. Dr. Stanilaus Swaminathan, SDB, principal, has been known for the high standards it has set for itself. I owe a deep sense of gratitude to him as it was he who groomed me to set my sight on this degree of academic excellence. He provided many valuable insights on theory, subject matter and analysis.

I sincerely thank the Management of Sacred Heart College, particularly Rev. Fr. Dr. Varghees, SDB, Rector, Rev. Fr. Antonyraj, SDB, Vice Principal, Rev. Fr. Maria Soosai, SDB, Vice-Principal (Evening College) who helped me in all possible ways to complete my Ph.D.work.

I also wish to express my sincere thanks to Dr. M. Ravichandran, Director, AICTE, Southern Region, Chennai-6, Dr. Nirmala Prasad, Principal, M.O.P. Vaishnav College, Chennai, Dr. N. Nishar Ahmed, Head, Department of

Corporate Secretaryship, Mazharul Uloom College, Ambur, Dr. Shrimathy Ramalingam, Lecturer, Department of Commerce, Pachiyappas College for Women, Kancheepuram, who provided me timely guidance and encouragement.

I owe a deep sense of gratitude to my mentor Mr. V. Jayaraman, IFS, Chief Conservator of Forest (Rtd.), Govt. of India, as it was he who groomed me to set my sight on this degree of academic excellence.

My sincere gratitude is due to Dr. N.P. Srinivasan, M.Com., M.Phil., Ph.D., former HOD of Commerce, University of Madras, for his kindness in writing the foreword for this book.

I wish to express my sincere and wholehearted thanks to respectful Mr. KMG. Subramaniyan, B.A., Vice Chairman, and Mr. KMG. Rajendiran, B.Sc., B.L., Joint Secretary, KMG College of Arts and Science, Gudiyattam, for their appreciation and earnest support given to me in writing this book.

I sincerely thank the Management of Tirupattur Arts and Science College, particularly Mrs. Eswary Ponnusamy, Correspondent, and Mr. G. Ponnusamy, B.E., Principal, Tirupattur Polytechnic, who helped me in all possible ways for granting permission to complete my Ph.D. work.

My special thanks to Mr. A.S. Govindan, M.A., M.Ed., M.Phil., P.G. Asst. in Economics, Govt. Hr. Secondary School, Pudupettai, Rev. Fr. Maria Antony, SDB, and Dr. S.M. Krishnan, M.Com., M.Phil., M.Ed., Ph.D., Lecturers, Sacred Heart College, Tirupattur, who helped me in the collection of data in connection with my study.

I must acknowledge and express my deep sense of gratitude to the manufacturers, dealers and consumers of durable goods who unflinchingly responded readily to my questionnaire used for the study.

All the members of the staff of Tirupattur Arts and Science College, Tirupattur, assisted me in one way or other during the course of the preparation of the thesis. My colleagues in the Department of Commerce, Mrs. V.

Vijayalakshmi, M.Com., M.Phil., Mrs. D. Tamilzharasi, M.B.A., and Mr. V. Paramasivan, M.A., M.Phil., who were of immense help, and took a lot of effort in connection with manscript and correction work.

My Sincere thanks are due to prof. V. Rahmatulla, Lecturer, Department of English, Islamiah College, Vaniyambadi, and Mrs. S. Amutha, Lecturer, Department of English, M.K.Jain College, Vaniyambadi, for his and her great help from the beginning till the end of the study.

I sincerely thank the staff of TCDS Computer Center at Jolarpettai, Advocate A. Gnanamohan, M.Com., M.Phil., LLB., Proprietor, Miss M. Suja, Miss. S. Samundeswari, Mr. T. Suresh, MCA., Miss. M. Bagyalakshmi, M.Com., and Miss. D. Anuradha, MCA., for the neat execution of the text through MS Word Processing.

My wife, N. Sengani, M.Com., M.Phil., B.Ed., who has been a source of inspiration, deserves a word of thanks. My beloved daughter Ms. V. Vaishali, and my son Mr. V. Vingnesh helped me by the supply of pencil, eraser etc. during my correction work. My thanks are due to each one of them.

I wish to express my regards to Mr. T. Anbu, M.A., M.Phil., Mr. S. Peter, M.Sc., M.Phil., Mr. M. Megarajan, M.A., M.Phil., and Mr. R. Babu Janarthanam, M.Sc., M.Phil., Lecturers, KMG College of Arts and Science, Gudiyattam, for their continuous encouragement in preparing this book.

A final word of thanks to the designers, Printers Publications, Serials Publications, New Delhi for bringing out this book neatly and successfully within a short time.

My success in this approach to a higher degree of academic excellence was made possible by a still larger number unnamed but not forgotten persons. I salute them and say may their tribe increase.

Last but not the least, I am indebted to my parents for their continuous encouragement and generous support, financial or otherwise during my years of formal education. The process of learning continues.

Dr. A. Vinayagamoorthy

Foreward

I am happy that Dr. A. Vinayagamoorthy, Lecturer Department of Commerce, Bharathiar University, Coimbatore-641 046, Tamil Nadu has come out with a book titled, 'Purchase Decision and Consumer Behaviour', for the benefit of the marketers, consumers, students and teachers both as a text book as well as a reference book. Dr. A. Vinayagamoorthy is a lucid writer and contributing his leisure time towards valuable publication of books in the field of commerce, marketing , management and accounting.

I have great pleasure in writing this foreword for the publication of this study by Dr. A. Vinayagamoorthy. Purchase Decision and Consumer Behaviour is a relatively new branch of commerce and marketing, hardly five decades old. Consumer behaviour was a new field of study in the mid 1960s. The new discipline, borrowed heavily from concepts developed in other scientific disciplines, such as, Psychology, Sociology, Social Psychology, Cultural Anthropology and Economics and Commerce. There are only few studies in the field in India. In this context, Dr. A. Vinayagamoorthy has made a useful contribution by studying various aspects of Purchase Decision and Consumer Behaviour of marketing in India. The study is based on the first hand personal field in investigations conducted by the author and it bears an imprint of tremendous amount of work resulting in an interesting analysis.

In order to be successful, a marketer is concerned with who is the consumer?. What do consumers buy?. When do consumers buy?. How do consumers buy?. From where do consumers buy?. Why do consumers buy?. Marketer, consumer, students, general public and decision makers are interested in these questions. They will surely find this study useful and interesting. I hope and wish that this book will be well received by the marketers, consumers, students and teachers.

(Dr. N.P. Srinivasan)

Ever grateful

to

My Parents

Late Mr. K. Anumuthan

And

Mrs. Rajammal Anumuthan

Dedicated to The Revered **Thirumigu Kalvithanthai K.M.Govindarajanar, Chairman, KMG Group of Institutions, Gudiyattam.** He is 86 years old freedom fighter and going tough in following Gandhian principles even at this age. He is a complete man in every aspect in Gudiyattam town. He is a successful industrialist, educationalist and a social worker. He is a man of courage, hard work and integrity. He served much of his life for the independence of our country.

1
Introduction

PURCHASE DECISION

In many purchase situations the consumer is confronted with a complex set of alternatives. He has to choose among a variety of products. From a variety of products, he makes selections, based on size, colour, style, models and brands. Also, the consumer can make decisions about when and where to buy a certain product, how much he wants to pay and how he will pay for it. Some purchase decisions are routine and may not require much attention. Some other purchase situations involving more cash outlays, safety and health have to be examined. Many product purchases require the evaluation of a variety of economic, social and psychological factors as by the consequences of a wrong decision can be costly.

The economic concept of consumers' sovereignty points out that consumer is a king in the market. According to this concept all the productive resources are deployed so as to fulfil the needs of the consumer. Consumers' tastes and choices are supposed to be fulfilled by the process of market forces. Is it so in reality?. There can be two explanations for such a reality. One is that the market forces and the laws of economics aim at fulfilling the needs and aspirations of the consumers at the macro level, and not at the micro level. That is to say that even though each and every need of the individual consumer is not fulfilled the general or overall trend in the consumer tastes and choices as reflected in the market trends are fulfilled by the market forces. Otherwise, markets cannot exist. The other explanation is based on the nature of markets in individual products and services. There are two types of markets-buyers market and sellers market. While in buyers market the consumers are supposed to have the upper hand and the products are designed to fulfil their needs and aspiration, in the latter, whatever is produced is sold and hence, there is no question of consumer needs.

MODELS OF CONSUMER BEHAVIOUR

Traditional Models of Consumers

The earliest comprehensive consumer models were actually devised by economists seeking to understand economic systems. Economics involves the study of how scarce resources are allocated among unlimited wants and needs[1]. Its two major disciplines- macroeconomics and microeconomics-have each developed alternative views of consumers, partially because they have undergone some modernization. These models still influence contemporary views of consumers.

Microeconomic Model

The classical microeconomic approach, developed early in the nineteenth century, focused on the pattern of goods and prices in the entire economy. It involved making a series of assumptions about the nature of the "average" consumer, and then developing a theory useful in explaining the working of an economy, made up of many such people. Focus was placed on the consumer's act of purchase, which, of course, is only a portion of what we have defined as consumer behaviour. Consumers develop various needs and preferences and how consumers rank these needs and preferences. Thus, micro economists concentrated on explaining what consumers would purchase, and in what quantities these purchases would be made. The tastes and preferences, leading to these purchases were assumed to be known already. Therefore, micro economists chose to ignore why consumers develop various needs and preferences and how consumers rank these needs and preferences.

Economists argued that perfect rational consumers will always purchase the good that provides them with the highest ratio of additional benefit to cost. For any given good, this benefit/cost ratio can be expressed as a ratio of its marginal utility to price (MU/P). Therefore, it can be shown that the consumer would seek to achieve a situation where the following expression holds for any number (n) of goods:

$$\frac{MU_1}{P_1} = \frac{MU_2}{P_2} = \frac{MU_3}{P_3} = \ldots\ldots\ldots\ldots = \frac{MU_n}{P_n}$$

If any one product's ratio is greater than the others, the consumer can achieve greater satisfaction per dollar from it and will immediately purchase more of it. Provided there is an adequate budget, the consumer will continue purchasing until the product's declining marginal utility reduces its MU/P ratio to a position equal to all other ratios. Additional purchasing of that good will then stop.

Macroeconomic Viewpoints

Macroeconomics focuses on aggregate flows in the economy – the monetary value of goods and resources, where they are directed, and how they change over time[2]. From such a focus, the macroeconomist draws conclusions about the behaviour of consumers who influence these flows. Although, the discipline has not generated a full-unified model of consumers, it does offer a number of insights into their behaviour.

One interest centers on how consumers divide their income between consumption and savings. This deals with two economic facts of life; higher-income families spend a smaller proportion of their disposable income than do lower-income families, but, as economic progress, all income levels over time these proportions do not seem to change. That is, lower-income groups do not significantly change the proportion of income devoted to spending as economic progress results in an increase in their income. The relative-income hypothesis explains this apparent contradiction by arguing that their peers and social groups rather than their absolute income levels mainly influence people's consumption standards. Therefore, the proportion of a family's income devoted to consumption is expected to change only when an income change places the family in a different social setting. This will not happen when all income levels are rising at the same time.

Another macroeconomic proposition, the permanent-income hypothesis, explains why specific individuals are slow to change their consumption patterns even when their incomes do suddenly change. It proposes that consumers do not use actual income in any period to determine the amount of their consumption expenditures, but instead are influenced by their estimate of some average, long - term amount that can be consumed without reducing their accumulated wealth[3]. Sudden increases or decreases in income are viewed by the consumer as temporary, and therefore, are expected to have little influence on consumption activity.

A variety of other variables have been suggested by macroeconomists as influencing consumption patterns. Included are consumers' previous income experiences, accumulated liquid assets, and variations in taxes or credits. Although useful, these suggestions represent rather traditional approaches to studying consumers, stressing economic variables while tending to ignore the influence of psychological factors.

Behavioural Economics

As mentioned earlier, traditional economics focused on the results of economic behaviour (supply, quantity demanded, prices and the like) rather than the actual behaviour of consumers themselves. Behavioural influences on consumers were viewed as complicating factors, which could be assumed to cancel each other out. George Katona found this approach lacking, and argued that an appreciation of how psychological variables influence consumers could lead to a deeper understanding of the behaviour of economic agents[4]. Katona's viewpoint, now known as behavioural economics, was fostered by important changes, which occurred in our economy, especially after World War II. Rising income levels had given a large number of consumers' significant discretionary income – spending power available after necessities had been purchased. In short, our economy had changed from one characterized as "much for a few" to one described as" more for many"[5].

What made discretionary income so interesting to Katona and others is that it has become a very important component of our economic system since a healthy portion of it is devoted to the purchase of durable goods such as cars, stereos, washing machines, and compact disk players. Because, the cost of these items is usually high, consumers will tend to purchase them when they perceive the general economic climate and their personal situation as being favorable. Therefore, this important influence on our economy is somewhat volatile and is affected by consumers' perceptions and economic expectations.

Katona's behavioural economics perspective is shown in figure 1.1.below

Fig.1.1: Katona's Behavioural Economics Perspective

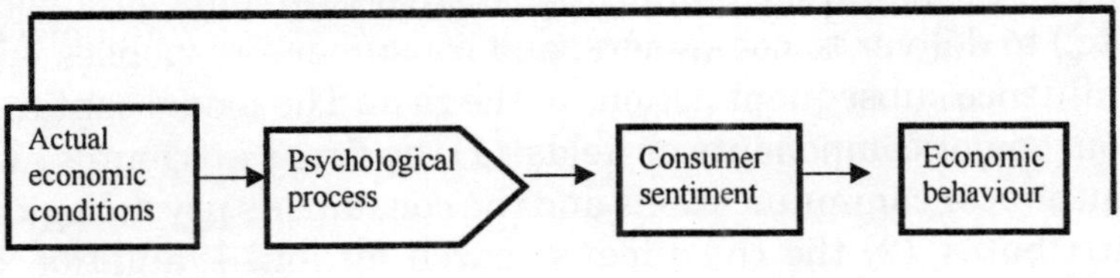

Contemporary Models

As the study of consumer behaviour evolved into a distinct discipline, newer approaches were offered to describe and explain what influenced consumer behaviour. These contemporary views are quite different from previous models because of their concentration on the decision process that consumers engage in when deliberating about products and services. Therefore, contrary to the economic models, emphasis is placed on the mental activity that occurs before, during, and after purchases are made.

A second distinguishing characteristic of contemporary models is their extensive borrowing from material developed in the behavioural sciences. In fact, most of the variables discussed in these models were originally identified in the fields of psychology and sociology.

A large number of contemporary consumer models have been developed, varying considerably in terms of their sophistication, precision, domain, and scope. A few of the more widely quoted models are presented here.[6]

Nicosia Model

Francesco Nicosia was one of the first consumer-behaviour modelers to shift focus from the act of purchase itself to the more complex decision process that consumers engage in about products and services[7]. He presented his model in flow-chart format, resembling the steps in a computer program. Also, all variables are viewed as interacting, with none being inherently dependent or independent. Thus, the model describes a circular flow of influences where each component provides input to the next.

The model is viewed as representing a situation where a firm is designing communications (advertisements, products, etc.) to deliver to consumers, and consumer's responses will influence subsequent actions of the firm. The model contains four major components or fields: (1) the firm's attributes and outputs or communications and the consumer's psychological attributes, (2) the consumer's search for and evaluation of the firm's output and other available alternatives, (3) the consumer's motivated act of purchase, and (4) the consumer's storage or use of the product. Nicosia assumes that the consumer is seeking to fulfil specific goals and that initially there is no history between the consumer and the firm, so no positive or negative predispositions toward the firm exist in the consumer's mind.

Howard-Sheth Model

The Howard- Sheth model serves as an integrating framework for a very sophisticated comprehensive theory of consumer behaviour[8]. It should be noted that the authors actually use the term "buyer" in their model to refer to industrial purchases as well as ultimate consumers. Thus, it can be seen that their interest was to develop a unified theory, useful for understanding a great variety of behaviours.

The model attempts to depict rational brand choice behaviour by buyers under conditions of incomplete information and limited abilities. The model borrows from learning-theory concepts to explain brand choice behaviour over time as learning takes place and the buyer moves from extensive to routinized problem-solving behaviour. Four major components are involved: (1) input variables, (2) output variables, (3) hypothetical constructs and (4) exogenous variables.

Engel-Blackwell-Miniard Model

The Engel - Blackwell- Miniard model was originally developed in 1968 by Engel, Kollat, and Blackwell, and has gone through numerous revisions[9].

Most recently, Miniard has contributed the model in conjunction with Engel and Blackwell[10]. It stands as one of the most popular representations of consumer behaviour.

The scheme depicts consumer behaviour as a decision process of five activities which occur over time: (1) motivation and need recognition, (2) search for information, (3) alternative evaluation, (4) purchase, and (5) outcomes. As shown in the model, variables are grouped into four general categories (a) stimulus inputs, (b) information processing, (c) decision process, and (d) variables influencing the decision process.

These models are intended to explain certain key aspects of buyer behaviour. The behaviour models naturally serve as a guide for research design and analysis. For the marketing manager, such models can provide a predictive analytical tool for a more effective mix of product, distribution and communication strategies.

Consumer Behaviour

The term consumer behaviour is defined as the behaviour that consumers display in 'searching for, purchasing, using, evaluating, and disposing of products, services and ideas which they expect will satisfy their needs'. The study of behavioural aspects of consumers is the study of how individuals take decisions in spending their available resources -money, time, efforts-on consumption related items. It includes the study of what they buy, why they buy, how they buy, when they buy, where they buy, and how often they buy it?.

Consumption affects our lives through either our own actions or those of other consumers. It has got a great deal of practical relevance to our daily living. Thus, consumer behaviour refers to acts of individuals directly involved in obtaining and using economic goods and services,including the decision making process that precedes to determine these acts. Consumer behaviour is an integral factor in the ebb and flow of all business in a consumer – oriented society.[7]

In order to be successful, a marketer is concerned with who is the consumer? . What do consumer buy? . When do consumers buy? . How do consumers buy? . From where do consumers buy? . Why do consumers buy? . Peter F. Drucker is of the opinion that "it is the consumer who determines what a business is... what it produces and whether it will prosper. The importance of consumption was recognized even in early periods, or at least two hundred years ago, when Adam Smith stated that consumption is the sole purpose of all production".

Consumer behaviour was a new field of study in the mid to late 1960s. The new discipline borrowed heavily from concepts developed in other scientific disciplines, such as psychology, sociology, social psychology, cultural anthropology and economics.

When the consumer evaluates the consequences of his purchase decisions, he may perceive some degree of 'perceived risk'. Where the degree of risk felt is large, the purchase may, perhaps, be cancelled or postponed. In such cases, the consumer may have the option to reduce his perceived risk through search and acquisition of additional information prior to purchase.

Decision Process

There are five stages in the buying decision process...

1. Problem recognition (need arousal), 2. Information search (identification of alternatives), 3. Evaluation of alternatives (evaluation of different brands), 4. Purchase decision (taking a final decision), and 5.

Post – Purchase behaviour (feed back information i.e., Post-Purchase feelings of satisfaction or dissatisfaction).[11]

The decisions, consumers take in connection with purchases, are influenced by various factors[12]. The major factors which influence consumer behaviour are.... 1. Culture, 2. Sub-culture, 3. Social class and 4. Personal factors which are presented in Fig. 1.2.

Decision Making Process

Deciding what to buy is one of the consumer's most basic tasks. No buying activity may take place unless this fundamental decision is made. A consumer's product or service decision may encompass not only the generic category of products desired, such as appliances, but more specifically, the narrower range of items, such as kitchen appliances. Consumers must even make decisions on brands, prices, and products features.

The study broadly aims at examining perceptions of the consumers mainly in terms of the information gathered and used for the purpose of the ultimate purchase decision. The pre-purchase behaviour of the consumers and a list of specific factors, which are considered as the evaluation criteria, constitute the basic data for the study. In this process, the

Fig. 1.2 : A Simplified Decision-Process Framework For Studying Consumer Behaviour

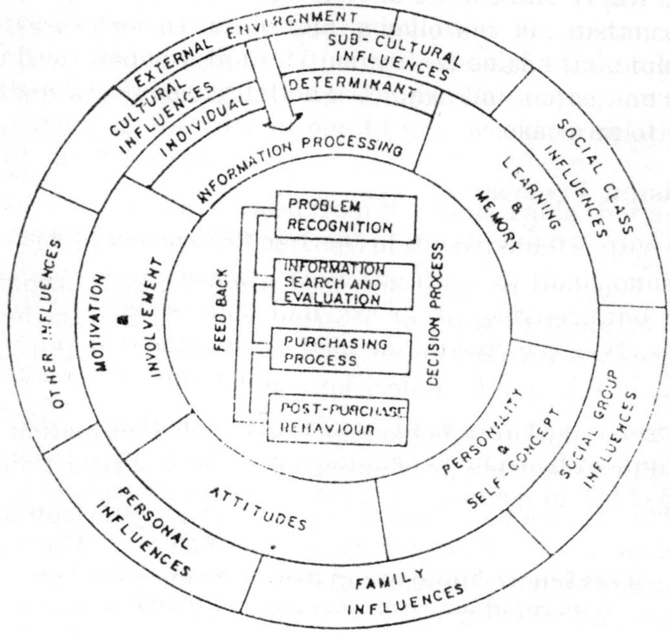

goods with reference to which the information relates to are four viz., television, refrigerator, air-cooler and washing machine.

STATEMENT OF THE PROBLEM

Attitudes have been used widely ranging from predicting consumer choice behaviour to serving as a basis of market segmentation, which requires quantitative measurement of consumer responses to various attitude dimensions, resulting in clustering of respondents by their attitude. Very few studies have been carried out to find out the process by which these attitudes are formed, a process that underlies important phenomena of attitude structure and change.

By understanding how the consumer forms a purchasing decision i.e., the sources he may rely for evaluation of information and the product attributes, he will consider as important will help the marketers to predict the brand, the consumer may choose, and if there exists homogeneous groups, marketers can also segment the market, either on the basis of the psychological characteristics or product attributes in order to better reach the target market.

In the eighties, India got a whiff of liberalization, which in turn aided her to usher in a new era of consumerism. A whole range of consumer durables started flooding the markets. Televisions, washing machines, videocassette recorders, durable products etc., which were the preserve of upper class during the seventies, have suddenly started thronging the middle-income group households. The focus of everyone's attention has shifted to owning these gadgets, and the very social status of the family has come to be assessed by the possession of these assets. A noteworthy development of the eighties is that even the low-income groups have started acquiring a wide range of consumer durables.

Consumer Durables

Television

One of the wonders of science, by sitting at a place, one can see what is going on around the world. The world has become very short and small. The saying, "seeing is believing", is true. This is helpful to communicate to one another. Thus the television media plays a vital role in present day humanity, and it has, become part and parcel of modern living. It has become essential item and not a luxurious one.

The television ramifications like cable television, videotapes, compact disk, internet and such other things have become inseparable part of human life. Then the student community was able to enrich their knowledge through these videotapes. The scientific benefit on the health side is innumerable. For instance, medical prescriptions can be obtained over internet for a patient in a remote village from any part of the world.

Refrigerator

The refrigerator products are one of the first household items to be purchased by the booming middle class. On account of the tropical climate in India, foodstuffs, particularly perishables deteriorate faster in quality. As more and more women take up jobs, households look out for appliances that can save time and cost. A durable product, in these situations becomes an essential commodity for a household. While the durable products passed from mere luxury items to an essential day-to-day commodity, its marketing has become more and more aggressive. Like refrigerator, all other three products for the study viz., (television, washing machine and air cooler) are also considered as common and essential commodities for every household today.

In nature, many of the harvested produce requires a constant local climate to remain sound. Milk, flowers, vegetables, human blood etc., cannot, on their own, remain sound with out the refrigerator. Such life saving items are made available in their original form through this machine. This brings out the importance of refrigerator. Knowing the importance, Governments have created food technology, food preservation units and dairy.

Despite these developments in the country, research in consumer behaviour has been largely concentrated on single measure of decision making that too on non-durable and agrarian products, that limits the generalizability of the finding.

Air-Cooler

In nature, all living beings are conditioned to live in a particular atmosphere, humanity is destined by nature a body temperature of 98.6 Fahrenheit. A tolerable fluctuation, say 4 or 5 Fahrenheit, we are able to go about. Beyond this, in order to carry on our activities, the science invented cooling mechanism, microclimate by air cooler machines etc. The air conditioner even at present with all innovations is beyond the reach of common man. Air cooler is less costly, and is available at affordable price. It is a portable one, in moving vehicles also. It is no more a luxury, and it is essential, especially during summer. Even where air conditioner is not possible to operate upon patients, this comes as handy. The operation of this machine, besides bringing down the temperature, prevents the skin eruptions, mental tension and precipitation.

Washing Machine

It is the process of mechanization of washing. The amount of manual labour will not commensurate with the out - turn of manual labour in these aspects. To the human labour, time, energy, cost is made up with more results through this machine. One has to go near water source for washing, which is unnecessary by this invention, whereby, washing is made possible in any floor of any multi-storied building. This also does not pollute the atmosphere. The office going people find this machine very handy, as it does not affect their duties. The machine has progressed to the extent of drying and giving the clothes in a perfect condition automatically. This machine is no longer a luxury, no longer a possession of the rich, and no longer unaffordable one. This is forming a part and parcel of modern living. The everlasting scientific pursuit may bring more wonders in these aspects.

THE NEED AND IMPORTANCE OF INFORMATION

The importance of per-purchase information in consumer evaluations of products and brands is well documented. How many sources of information do consumers consult before they buy?. Do the sources vary in number in terms of products?. Which source of information is considered by the consumer at the time of making the final decision?. What factors the consumer considers at the time of making his choice?.

The study of behavioural aspects of consumers is of great importance for marketers and this knowledge is applied to find out the consumers' wants and needs. In India, consumer legislations, since, 1960 have created special interest in this subject. The main point for developing successful marketing strategy is a clear understanding of the consumers' mind before, during and after a purchase. As all consumers are not alike and their preferences are constantly changing, they prefer differentiated products, which reflect their own special needs, personalities and lifestyles.

The study aims at finding answers to such questions in respect of buyers of durable goods like television, refrigerator, washing machine and air cooler. The consumer's information problem arises because the search process generally must precede the purchase. A consumer with high information requirements will presumably invest more effort into his search. If information is not readily available to that consumer, his effort might be directed at finding more information.

If such information is accessible to that consumer, his search effort may consist in sorting out those clues that are relevant to him. The information may also be confusing when messages from different sources contradict each other or the consumer's prior experience with a particular brand or product. A consumer with low information requirements may be presumed to spend less effort in his search.

To provide the consumer with market transparency, he needs guidelines and product information. Business critics have long maintained that consumer is lacking that information, and as a consequence, he is ill equipped to make intelligent choices. Once product information has been acquired through search, the consumer must evaluate competing alternatives to arrive at a purchase decision.

This involves the interaction of different factors like price, brand popularity, availability of the product, reputation, and location of the dealer, technical performance, size, colour, design etc. Based on the evaluation of important factors, the consumer makes a purchase decision. The decision is made on the basis of the consumer's perception.

THE INDIAN CONSUMER

In applying the theories to understand the behavioural dynamics of the Indian consumer, one has to be cautious. Most of the buyer behaviour models and findings have been developed with the sophisticated western buyer as the focus. But to understand the peculiarities of the Indian consumer, to construct his buying profile, he has to be studied in relation to his environment, his culture and tradition, his educational and economic status, his level of exposure, and the degree of his sophistication. Academic institutions and individual researchers have conducted a few studies on isolated aspects of the buying behaviour of the Indian consumer.

Indians as a class present a striking contrast to the people of the West. By and large, they are not an adventurous thrill seeking, highly-strung community. Basically, they are conservative minded and tradition bound people. They are contended with the small happenings in the family or community. These are some general characteristics of the Indian consumer, but it does not mean that Indians are homogeneous people, fitting into a common characteristic. Due to the diversity in religion and caste, languages and cultural style, it will be more practicable to classify the Indian consumer on the basis of his economic status, as the rich class consumer, the middle class consumer and the lower class consumer. It is the middle class that constitutes the largest consuming sector for manufacturing goods in the country today. For any marketer in the country, this group offers the maximum scope, and the maximum demand potential.

OBJECTIVES OF THE STUDY

The overall objective of the present study is to analyse the purchase decision and consumer behaviour with reference to the consumers of selected durable goods in Vellore district of Tamil Nadu. The specific objectives of the study are enunciated below.

(i) To examine the relative importance of the information sources used by the consumers in the purchase of four consumer durable products.

(ii) To find out the differences between the users and non-users of the particular sources of information in the search process and the dependency of certain selected variables.

(iii) To analyse the evaluation criteria used in making the final decision, and

(iv) To identify the factors influencing the consumers in the decision–making process.

With the above objectives, this study would be able to provide an outline of the information gathering process and factors considered in the alternate evaluation by consumers and thus contribute to a better understanding of the subject in the Indian context.

SIGNIFICANCE OF THE STUDY

This study deals with certain aspects of the pre-purchase behaviour of selected Indian consumers of four consumer durables, viz., television, refrigerator, washing machine and air-cooler. It is concerned with the search for and use of product information, as a part of purchase decision making, which concerns consumer reaction to alternate product information sources.

The study identifies and analyses the factors that influence purchase decision. The present study is an attempt to add to the existing knowledge in the Indian context. The consumerist issue directly affects all participants in the market place and should be of great interest to students of marketing as well as marketers.

The study also deals with the amount of information gathered by the Indian consumers at the time of search process, and how effectively they use the information in making a purchase. There are different sources of product information available to a prospective consumer. What are the sources, he gathered and used for a purchase decision is of great importance. The relative importance of information sources may vary from product to product according to the consumer's own perceptions. At the time of making the choice, the consumer usually has different alternatives. He has to evaluate these different alternatives, which he gathered in the search process. The evaluation of alternatives requires the interaction of several factors. The importance of these factors may vary from product to product and consumer to consumer.

LIMITATIONS OF THE STUDY

The details about the consumer's behaviour could be gathered only from 450 sample consumers out of the 600 samples chosen for the study. The 25 per cent of the sample respondents failed to return the questionnaires. It limits the scope of the study of 450 sample consumers.

1. The sample of 450 consumers represents a cross section of the total population.
2. The study focused attention on only three categories of information sources, as used by the consumers, as follows:
   - (i) Personal sources of information: this source includes friends, relatives, one's own past experience with the product.
   - (ii) Commercial source: this source includes advertisements through mass media, and
   - (iii) Retail outlet sources: this source includes shop visits and retail outlets.
3. Attention is given only to fifteen variables, which are considered most common in the alternate evaluation process.
4. The study focuses its attention only on two stages in consumer decision-making behaviour viz., search and alternative evaluation. The other stages are not considered in this study, as it would add to its volume.

ORGANIZATION OF CHAPTERS

The report is presented in *Seven Chapters. The First Chapter* introduces the subject matter and set out the problems, objectives, significance and limitations of the study.

Chapter II relates to the review of literature and basic concepts used in the study.

Chapter III provides the profile of the study area, Vellore District.

Chapter IV deals with the methodology of the study.

Chapter V analyse the relative importance of the three information sources used by the consumers, the differences between the users and non-users of the particular sources of information with reference to selected variables, the evaluation criteria used in making the final decision.

Chapter VI deals with the factors, influencing the Consumer's decision-making process.

Chapter VII Summarizes the major findings of the study.

Bibliography

REFERENCES AND NOTES

1. Michael J. Brennan, (1965),"Theory of Economic Statics", Prentice–Hall, Englewood Cliffs, NJ, p.4.
2. Richard H.Leftwich, (1966),"The Price System and Resource Allocation", Holt, New York, (3 rd ed.,) p.8.
3. Milton Friedman, (1957), "A Theory of the Consumption Function", Princeton University Press, Princeton, NJ, and J.William Levedahl, June (1980), "The Impact of Permanent and Transitory Income on Household Automobile Expenditures", *Journal of Consumer Research,* pp.7.55 – 66.
4. George Katona, (1963),"The Relationship Between Psychology and Economics", in S.Koch (ed.), Psychology: A Study of A Science. McGraw Hill, New York, p. 603.
5. George Katona, (1980)," Essasy on Behavioural Economics", University of Michigan, Ann Arbor, p.6.
6. Francesco M. Nicosia and Yoram Wind, (1977),"Behavioural Models for Market Analysis", Foundations for Marketing Action, *Dryden, Hindsdale, Gerald Zaltman and Melanie*

Wallendorf, (1979),"Consumer Behaviour": Basic Findings and Management implications, Wiley, New York, pp. 515–542; *Charles D.Schewe,* July (1973),"Selected Social Psychological Models for Analyzing Buyers "Journal of Marketing, 37:31 – 39; *Philip Kotler,* October (1965) "Behavioural Models for Analyzing Buyers, "Journal of Marketing , 29:37 – 45; *John A. Howard and Jagdish N.Sheth,* (1969), "The Theory of Buyer Behaviour Wiley" ,New York ,p.605 and *Jagdish N.Sheth,* (1974),"Models of Buyer Behaviour"; Conceptual ,Quantitative & Empirical Harper & Row, New York, p. 606.

7. Franceso Nicosia, (1966), "Consumer Decision Processes": Marketing and Advertising Implications, Prentice–Hall, Englewood Cliffs, NJ. p. 605.
8. John A. Howard and Jagdish N. Sheth, (1969),"The Theory of Buyer Behaviour", Wiley, New York, p.607.
9. James F.Engel, David T. Kollat, and Roger D.Blackwell (1968),"Consumer Behaviour", Holt, Rinehart and Winston, New York, p. 610.
10. James F.Engel David T.Kollat And Roger D.Blackwell, (1990) "Consumer Behaviour", The Dryden Press, Chicago, (6th Ed.), p. 610.
11. Philip Kotler, (1984), "Marketing Management–Analysis, Planning and Control", Prentice–Hall of India, New Delhi, (5th ed.), p.147.
12. David L. London and Alberet J. Della Bitta, (2002), Consumer Behaviour", Concept and Applications, Tata McGraw Hill, New Delhi, (4th ed.) p.3-51.

2

Review of Literature and Basic Concepts

EVOLUTION OF CONSUMER INFORMATION IN ECONOMIC THOUGHT

The classical model of economic man assumes a consumer who can state his preferences; who is consistent in his choice, and who is rational in his behaviour. Endowed with perfect knowledge of the market offering, this economic consumer is capable of maximizing his subjective utility function with mathematical precision, subject only to his budget constraint[1]. Frank Knight introduced risk and uncertainty into economic thinking[2], and Von Neumann and Morgenstern formally incorporated[3] these concepts into the theory of consumer behaviour. The consumer now maximizes not merely utility, but he maximizes "expected" utility[4].

The probabilistic model of Von Neumann and Morgenstern clearly implies imperfect knowledge on the part of consumers. But Stigler treated information explicitly on cost in applying marginal analysis to the search process[5]. In his theory on the "Economics of Information", Stigler hypothesized that an individual will continue his information search as long as the incremental value gain per unit of search is grater than the marginal cost associated with it. The optimal information point is established when the marginal value of information equals the marginal cost of search. The consumer, in terms of lower prices and better quality from which he presumably obtains greater utility, assesses the value gained from each search effort. The cost of information is measured in time units, effort, and money associated with the search. Stigler's theory would predict, for example, an individual with high income would spend less time and effort on information search than another with low income. Studies have shown that neither the high nor low income brackets will seek much information in buying durable products, but that the middle income groups are acquiring information most actively[6].

The Swedish economist, Staffan Linder, explains this seeming contradiction by noting that, with rising income, the number of consumption decisions increases too. High-income people have also greater demand on their scarce time. The combination of these simultaneous phenomena leads, Linder to the thesis of "a declining quality of decisions", which fits the high-income earners well. As regards the poor, "their low level of education means a low yield on time spent in the collection of information"[7].

Economic thinking has come a long way from the early models of economic man, although some of the classical notions seem to persist. But with Stigler and Linder, the stage is set for a closer look at the role of information in the marketing literature.

THE ROLE OF INFORMATION IN MARKETING

To the extent that marketing originated from economics, it suffered from unrealistic assumptions on the classical economic theory. Over the years, the study of marketing has been variously approached from institutional, commodity, functional and managerial standpoint[8].

More recently, the social approach to marketing has developed in which theories of group behaviours and interaction are used to explain markets and market behaviour[9]. Today, marketing is considered to be an eclectic discipline, borrowing freely from many fields such as psychology, social psychology, sociology and anthropology.

The purpose is to explore phenomena to understand and predict behaviours in market. The consumer's search for evaluation and use of information has become an integral area of inquiry within the study of consumer behaviour and marketing.

BUYER BEHAVIOUR MODELS

The aspects of search and use of consumer information are often treated as part of complex buyer behaviour or decision-making models. Howard[10] made the first articulate attempt to associate human behaviour with the buying process. He viewed buying as a process of learning. In choosing products and brand, an individual tends to rely strongly on his experience, (i.e. on what he has learned) but due to dynamically changing environment, the individual is required to continuously adapt his behaviour to these environmental changes by engaging in new learning. Depending on his experience, a buyer is positioned in various phases of the learning curve.

Accordingly, he engages in extensive problem solving, limited problem solving, or automatic response behaviour. In each of these progressive phases, there exists a gradually increasing amount of experience (i.e. stored prior learning) which is coupled with a declining amount of information seeking, that is, in any given purchase situation, the greater the experience with the particular products, the less will be the importance attached to outside sources of information such as advertising, discussion with friends and shopping guides.

Nicosia Decision Model

Nicosia's decision model includes a greater number of variables, and it is considerably more complex than that of Howard[11]. The exposure of an individual to an informational cue (e.g. an advertising message) may induce him to form certain attitudes. Search and the evaluation of means-ends relationships may motivate him to make the eventual purchase decision. In the process, consumers "attributes" are transformed from predisposition, to attitudes, to motivations. The transformation occurs through a combination of messages from various information sources, environmental situation and experience.

Engel's Purchasing Decision Model

Engel's purchasing decision model is quite similar to Nicosia's model and includes stages for the search and evaluation of alternatives (i.e. information seeking). At each stage of the process, the consumer is faced with a new decision, and he makes these decisions in the light of information which he passively receives or actively seeks, and which he then compares with his internal information (i.e. experience). The entire decision process takes place in what Engel calls the "central control unit"[12]. These models are intended to explain certain key aspects of buyer behaviour. For the researcher, behaviour models may serve as a guide for research design and analysis. For the marketing manager, such models can provide a predictive analytical tool for a more effective mix of product, distribution and communication strategies.

MARKET INFORMATION

Marketing implications of consumer behaviour models are abound[13]. Conclusions are drawn from the analytical framework provided by these models, such as how people arrive at purchase decisions, how they react to a new product or advertising message. For example, management's desire to predict and measure the effectiveness of the firm's communications mix has always been a continuous problem.

Lavidge and Steiner proposed much a model for the predictive measurement of advertising effectiveness[14]. They postulated that potential buyers must first be made aware of the existence of a product. During the decision process the individual moves from awareness to the ultimate purchase of the product along cognitive, affective and conative dimension of behaviour. They hypothesized that each step of the decision process requires different kinds of information and that advertising, which helps move people through the decision stages, can be designed accordingly to be either information or to induce attitude changes, or to directly stimulate desires for a particular product. One major purpose of their model was to predict and measure advertising effectiveness at each stage of the process, a procedure which they claimed was superior to the conventional advertising-sales measure.

The general concept of a "hierarchy of effects" as suggested by Lavidge and many authors have refined Steiner. Copland visualized the decision stages in terms of increasing purchase probabilities[15]. But as a tool for measuring advertising effectiveness, Palda criticized the 'hierarchy of effects' as suggested by Lavidge and Steiner and asked whether it is "... really more difficult and expensive to investigate the direct link between advertising expenditures and sales than it is to undertake research into each step of the hierarchy-even if the existence of a hierarchy were actually established"[16]. In another study by the same author, he had developed a model for measuring the cumulative effects of advertising based on multiple regression analysis[17].

Communication is the process of transmitting information. From the managerial view point, communications directed at consumers are designed in terms of promotional strategies, target markets, goals and objectives and budgets[18] It appears that much of the communication literature in marketing is written from the firm's standpoint, in that the implications are managerially oriented towards increased profitability and sales. The studies on advertising effectiveness are no exception. Their purpose is to aid management in the structuring of more effective communications and promotional mixes in order to increase a company's market share. The consumer's informational needs are not of their concern. For the purpose of this dissertation, one must look at some studies, which are concerned with the problem of information from the consumer viewpoint.

In studies concerning the use and usefulness of consumer information, the experimental approach has been widely employed. For example, Anderson and others reported experiments on the relationship between product proliferation and information value[19]. They found, first, that as the number of brands in a purchase decision increases, the consumer becomes less aware of and less sensitive to changes in any of the brands involved in the decision. Secondly, they found that with the increasing number of brands, the information for each item appeared to decline. They concluded that:... as the number of choices increases, the purchase decision becomes more difficult. That is, the added advantage of new sources of information for a purchase decision is outweighed by the disadvantages of added time and effort involved in the decision[20].

This conclusion seems to support Stigler's theory[21]. The results from the Anderson experiments also suggest that increased amounts of information may only be part of the solution to the consumer problem. The study indicates that "... as the consumer makes purchase decisions in the situations where there is a large number of choices, he experiences a considerable degree of anxiety, discomfort...[22]" At the same time, the post-purchase dissonance was greater, the greater the number of possible choices from alternative brands. The frustrations resulting from the market complexity, which was stimulated, in the experiment through an increasing number of brands from which subjects were forced to choose could not be alleviated fully by providing new information on these brands.

RISK AND THE BAYESIAN APPROACH

Edwards reported several experiments that dealt with acquisition and use of information. He attempted to compare the 'real with ideal' performance as based on the Bayesian decision model and found that the subjects tended to show a "qualitative correspondence" with the Bayesian model[23]. Paul Green conducted experiments in which he also related, "information buying" to the Bayesian model[24]. He found that the subjects were sensitive to differences in prior probabilities, but their behaviour was relatively insensitive to differences in information reliability and pay-offs. When there was no conflict between prior and sample information, subjects consistently chose in accordance with the Bayesian model. The experimental results of both Edwards and Green would seem to indicate that too much information can be as dysfunctional as too little information.

Closely related to Baysian approach is Bauer's view of the product choice process as a risk-taking situation where the consumer can obtain information at a cost in order to reduce his perceived risk of making a wrong decision[25] The higher the degree of perceived risk, the greater the likelihood of additional pre-purchase information search, and more the consumer is willing to expend in money, time and effort for additional information. Similarly, Green's experiments indicated that consumers tend to relate the cost of securing additional information to the weighted value of reducing the perceived cost of uncertainty[26].

THE NATURE OF INFORMATION SOURCES

Many authors have studied the effect of the nature of the source of information on consumer behaviour. Wilding and Bauer reported an experiment to test favourableness of attitude towards a communication source as related to personality variables[27].

Engel and others have studied the influence of information on the adoption of new 'self medication' products and they reported that the degree of influence depend on the seriousness of the ailment[28]. The television advertisements and discussion with friends were important sources of information at the bottom of their 'sickness scale' where minor ailments were involved.

Hempel conducted experimental studies of the effect of different types of information sources on consumer product evaluation[29]. Using two different brand shirts, he divided his subjects into a group, which expressed a preference for one brand name, and the second group preferring the other brand. He then presented each group with two divergent communications, (a) one message confirming prior preferences and (b) another message conflicting with it, from each of two information sources- consumer reports and a recorded sales talk. The members of each group, who were administered any two of the four possible 'message-information source' combinations, were randomly selected. From the resulting data, Hempel concluded that when both the messages confirmed the preferred brand, neither information source showed a significantly greater influence on the decision outcome. When one or both communications conflicted with prior brand preference, Consumer Reports appeared to have stronger effect on product choice than the recorded sales talk. Apparently, consumers tend to evaluate a piece of information not only by its content but also by the truth worthiness of its source.

There were several pieces of evidence available to support the possibility of distinctive search patterns. Kelman and Cohler suggested that cognitive needs and styles let to 'clarifiers' and 'simplifiers'[30]. Mueller noted that their findings seemed to indicate 'feature substitution' – through attention to some aspects of deliberation and limited attention to others[31]. Dommermuth found differences in search pattern by comparing numbers of store visit with number of brands considered[32]. At the individual buyer level, Cox reports clear differences in shopping patterns[33].

The study by Newmann and Staelin presents research findings which help to answer many questions such as how many sources of information do consumer consult before they buy? Do the sources vary in number and kind? What part does advertising play in the purchase decision process? [34]. The study, reported here, covered automobiles and six major appliances. The automobile and appliance data were analyzed separately and in the aggregate, by a multivariate technique as well as by frequency tables. Forty four percent of the buyers reported using only one type of source or none. Another forty four per cent used either two or three types of sources while twelve per cent used four or more. The findings for both automobiles and appliances were very similar. Some variation in number of sources was observed according to the type used. The number tended to be lower when source use included friends and neighbors and retail stores than when it included advertising or books, pamphlets and articles. The study did indicate, however that uses of different sources were positively inter-correlated. Use of each type of source was positively correlated with the use of each other type, as would be expected of measurements of the same construct. The highest correlation (0.44) was for advertising and books, pamphlets and articles, showing that users of advertising tend to seek out information in printed matter. The other correlations ranged from 0.108 to 0.235.

Newmann and Staelin also measured why some buyers use no more than one type of source, while others used several. To find out this, they used Automatic Interaction Detector (AID) computer programme to learn which of the 29 selected factors were most useful for segmenting the sample[35]. The programme sequentially produced binary splits of the respondents based on the combinations of levels of the independent variable, which minimized the within group sum of squares. The technique also detects interaction between variables.

One implication of the AID results was that consumers consider search cost and in many cases do not feel it worthwhile to contact several kinds of sources. Another implication of the findings was that consumer who presumably has the greatest need to use limited funds efficiently – i.e., households of lower education and income levels- are likely to seek and use information. Yet another finding of this study supports Bauer's view[36] that consumers are not passive receipients of commercial messages, but that they exercise initiative.

On the whole, Newmann and Staelin presented new empirical evidence of the use of information sources by users of consumer's durables. The findings disputed charges that advertisers monopolise the distribution of information and also claims that advertising supplies most of the information, people want before buying.

Comprehensive models of consumer behaviour have suggested that a consumers' past information is an important input into his brand choice[37, 38, 39]. These variables are generally thought to be one of the several key variables that intervene between a decision-maker's perceptions and his subsequent brand selection. Thus, knowledge of consumer's past information can help marketers influence brand choice.

Robert B.Woodruff in his article presented research focusing on the problems of measuring a consumer's past information about brand attributes[40]. A procedure for assessing consumer's prior brand information was discussed and observations were made with a sample of husbands and wives. Finally, suggestions were offered for improvement of the assessment procedure. The finding suggested that a consumer's prior information could be segregated by brands and attributes. However, separating prior information by attributes, requires that the assessment procedure allow a consumer to consider prior information about each brand's attributes separately, since his information about each brand or attributes is likely to be different. It was also suggested that measurement of consumer's prior information could be used effectively for basic research on business-consumer communication process. He also stated some examples of questions, guiding such research like: (a) which sources of information generally have the greatest impact on consumer groups of interest?, (b) what impacts do different kinds of appeals generally have on consumer brand decisions?, and (c) which information sources are most effective for each kind of appeal?[41] .

The research conducted by John D.Claston and others, employed numerical taxonomic analysis as a method for summarizing the ways in which shoppers gather information in purchasing durable goods-specifically furniture and appliances[42]. In this study, taxonomic numerical analysis proved to be useful for classifying buyer pre-purchase shopping behaviour. The primary purpose of the study was to analyse measures of pre-purchase search with a view to identifying patterns of information gathering and to assess the factors associated with differences in these patterns. Data for the study were obtained from personal interviews with 546 housewives. Questions dealing with five aspects of pre-purchase shopping activities were included in the questionnaire. They are type and range of alternatives considered, information source used, features considered, stores visited and time spent considering the purchase. These questions, of course, included in the earlier shopping behaviour studies conducted by Katona and Mueller[43], and Newmann and Staelin[44]. They concluded that three general clusters were identified in both furniture and appliance sample and were labelled – through (store intense), thorough (balanced) and non-thorough on the basis of group average measures in the discriminating variables. Within these groupings, sub-clusters varying in deliberation time were identified.

About five percent of qualifying furniture buyers were placed in the through (store intense) grouping. Their outstanding characteristics was making use of an average of twenty percent store visits in the purchasing process as compared with eight percent or less visits in other groups. The thorough (store intense) group also used more information sources (an average of more than three) and spent a longer time considering the purchase (almost an year). Forty four percent of the furniture buyers fell into second group-thorough (balanced). On the average, they consulted about three information sources, visited six stores and spent several months considering the purchase. Non-thorough buyers made up about thirty-four percent of furniture sample. On the average, they consulted only one source of information, two stores and deliberated on their purchase for only a few weeks.

In the sample of appliance buyers, about eight per cent were in thorough (store intense) grouping, and twenty-seven percent were in thorough (balanced) grouping. The lower number of information sources consulted by the store intense group as compared to the balance group may indicate a trade-off in mode of information gathering. The larger cluster was the non-thorough grouping, which took in about sixty-five percent of the appliance buyers. This basic grouping broke into three sub clusters, differentiated largely by deliberation time, again a pattern similar to that observed in the furniture results. In all sub-clusters, an average of only about one source of information was used, accompanied by only one store visit. The results by Claxton and others illuminate different approaches to the shopping task as identified by Katona and Mueller and Newmann and Staelin.

Newman and Staelin in another study used one more multivariate technique viz., Multiple Classification Analysis (MCA), dummy variable regression programme for examining the inter-relationship between independent variables and a dependent variable within the context of an additive model[45]. West Brook and Fornell, in their study, indicate that major appliance buyers can be classified according to distinctive patterns of pre-purchase information source usage, which are understandable in terms of various explanatory variables[46]. The variability in source usage noted by Newmann and Staelin[47] and the broad, overall pattern of search by Claxton and others[48] together suggested that distinctive patterns of source usage may characterize buyers of durable goods.

Some individuals may prefer to limit their pre-purchase search to certain kinds of sources, whereas others may choose to consult a wider variety of sources. The identification of such pattern would contribute to an improved understanding of the process of external pre-purchase information search. Because of this, Westbrook and Fornell to determine whether patterns of information source usage could be identified and related to selected explanatory variables undertook a study. The conceptual framework for the study provided three broad classes of variables, as potential determinants of information source usage patterns of durable goods buyers. They are (a) personal or background characteristics of consumers consisting of demographic descriptors such as age, education, and occupation, as well as satisfaction with the previous buying and ownership experience, (b) situational factors at the time of purchase including such variables as economic constraints, condition of previously purchased product (if any) and special opportunities to buy advantageously and (c) characteristics of consumer's purchase decision process consisting of internal factors such as size of the evoked set of brands, evaluative criteria, specific self confidence etc.

Data for the study were obtained by means of a telephone survey of major household appliances. Information source usage was determined by aided recall survey question, about the following pre-purchase activities viz., (1) visits to different retail outlets, (2) reading habits of books, pamphlets, magazine, newspapers and (3) seeking advice or opinion of friends, neighbors or relatives. These activities were termed as retail, neutral and personal sources of information respectively as mentioned by Newmann and Staelin[49]. The findings of the study indicate that major appliance buyers can be classified according to distinctive patterns of pre-purchase information source usage, which are understandable in terms of various explanatory variables. Classification was based on the identification of two underlying and independent dimensions of source usage: (1) extent of physical shopping and (2) use of neutral sources versus personal sources. The four segments, which emerged, were labelled objective shoppers, moderate shoppers, store intense shoppers and personal advice seekers. Age and education of the consumer, number of brands considered and working condition of a previously purchased product are related to segment membership. These results amplify the findings of Claxton and others[50] and offer more detailed insight into the morphology of consumer external search behaviour.

PAST STUDIES

The experimental studies reviewed have important implications for this study. They show that consumers confronted with alternatives, do perceive anxiety and may desire information in order to lower the risk of making a wrong decision. The greater the number of possible choices becomes, the more difficult is the decision, and the stronger may be the desire for additional information. Given additional information, consumers may, at some point, become prone to confusion instead of greater market transparency. The confusion arises, partly from the greater amount of information that they may have to process, and partly from the larger number of choices that may have to be made in a complex market environment. The limited time, which an individual consumer may be willing to devote to information search, can effectively reduce the informational input per decision as the number of alternatives increases. In such situations, consumers may revert back to simple forms of information, such as brand names and advertising.

Acquisition of information, active or passive, is a continuous process which can utilize many sources: experience, friends, retailers, quality seals, brand names, user's manuals, advertising and product testing and ranking publications. The experiments indicate, however, that people are often limited in their capacity to digest all the available information to sort it out, and to make best use of it for selecting and comparing alternatives. Information is often confusing, conflicting or technically beyond the understanding of many. From these arguments it follows that, although, consumers may attempt to lessen uncertainty through information acquisition, more information per se may neither help to actually reduce perceived risk prior to a decision, nor lower post-purchase dissonance in cases of high psychological commitment[51]. As Green has concluded...it is somewhat surprising that information revolution in which we are supposedly participating, provides little guidance about how consumers and managers do (or should) use the vast array of information. The process by which people selectively acquire and use information would thus seem to be an important area of research. If the capabilities and goals of human processes are ignored, the information revolution could simply result in more occasions for confusing the decision maker by offering him greater quantities of ambiguous, redundant or incorrect information[52].

The studies on consumer information, reviewed, above, are subject to certain limitations. Due to their experimental nature, they may be lacking in "real world applicability." Whether the results of these experiments on information can be transferred to the true-to-life consumer world remains at least open to question.

SOURCES OF INFORMATION'S

Different authors under different groupings have discussed the various consumer information sources. According to Engel and others, information sources may be grouped as 1.Personal, 2.Market originating and 3. Consumer oriented information sources[53]. The characteristic features of these sources and their implications to consumer are discussed now.

Personal Information Sources

Personal information source includes the consumer's own experience and activities and the experience of others. He gains access to the latter through his non-commercial, personal relationship. The consumer's own experience can be viewed as a result of learning over time[54]. It is a valuable guide in deciding on an often-purchased and used product. Where a new product is involved no learning may have taken place, yet. With seldom-acquired items such as major durables, prior experience is likely to be inadequate or a reliable information source.

Often the consumer can supplement his own experience with the experience of others. Discussion with friends, neighbours, and relatives is an important source of information for many consumers. As many studies have shown, personal sources often play a determining part in the outcome of a purchase decision.

The following are the findings of the studies relating to personal sources information[55]. (i) Almost 50 percent of male and female students discussed clothing brands, styles, retail outlets and prices with their friends[56]. (ii) A study of the diffusion of a new product in a married students' apartment complex revealed that exposure to favourable word-of-mouth was found to increase the probability of purchase, while exposure to unfavourable comments decreased the probability[57]. (iii) Another study found that the source of information most frequently consulted by durable goods buyers was friends and relatives. ".... More than 50 per cent of the buyers turned for advice to acquaintances and in most instances also looked at durable goods owned by them. "Even more striking is the finding that one-third of durable goods buyers bought a brand or model that they had seen at someone else's house, often the house of relatives[58]. (iv) A study of consumer attitude towards health care found that largest segment of consumers state the most important reason for choosing their doctor was a recommendation by a friend or relative[59].

Other studies have also found personal communication source to be very important in the purchase of food items and cleaning agents, in motion picture selections, hairdo styles, makeup techniques[60], general fashion[61], dental product and service[62], farming practices[63], physicians[64], and man-made fabrics[65].

By gaining social approval before making a final decision, information search from personal sources can be viewed as risk reducing process[66]. The difficulty of using the experience of others as information sources lies in the fact that people differ in their concepts about performance and the quality-price relationship. Friends, relatives and neighbors may lack adequate product knowledge and their personal circumstances may differ. Also quality standards, especially those of service, often do not remain constant over time, rendering personal sources of information not much reliable or useful than one's own experience. Where the advice of 'experts' is available, however, this personal source can serve as a valuable information input into the purchase decision. Studies have shown that 'experts' are more likely to be considered as opinion leaders within their sphere of influence.

In the words of Rogers, the individuals acquire their expertise, because opinion leaders use more impersonal, technical, accurate and cosmopolitan sources of information than their followers...messages emanating from outside the social system are often but not necessarily, more technically accurate than one locality sources[67].

Opinion leadership refers to the degree to which a person is able to influence informally other peoples' behaviour in a designed way[68]. Opinion leaders are those persons who seem to possess an unusual degree of this ability. They can affect the behaviour of others toward products favourably or unfavourably. If they are satisfied with an idea or new product, they can almost assure its success. Opinion leadership is, however, informal leadership[69]. Opinion leaders rarely go about attempting to control the actions of others. Rather, opinion leadership is subtle. Persons interacting with each other are not always aware that they are influencing or being influenced[70]. Moreover, it is not necessary for persons to talk to others to influence their actions. However, the influence takes places verbally, visually, or both- it is nonetheless real. In extreme cases, it can make or break a firm's product.

Opinion leaders can be located in the population by the socio-metric or the self-designated techniques. Their influence is limited to one or a few related topics of interest about which they expose themselves to sources of information. Opinion leaders differ from non-leaders on a number of important dimensions and the former are more exposed to topic relevant mass media; they are more gregarious and more interested in the area of influence and they usually interact with persons of similar but slightly lower status.

Market Originating Information

The market itself contains a wealth of information that can serve the consumer in his decision-making. For instance, the design can critically influence a purchase decision, especially in matters of taste and aesthetic values.

Thus, in the selection of such items like jewellery and furniture, appearance often plays a dominant role. In relying on visual inspection, appearance can be misleading. For example, packing often makes a product appear more desirable on the supermarket shelf than it actually is, once unpacked at home.

Quality grades are important clues intended to aid consumers evaluate products such as milk, oil, fruits and vegetables. Quality grades insure minimum quality and size as established by government or quality control institutes. If the quality gradations are too numerous and fine, however, they may be of little use to consumers. For instance, the quality grades in opticals, leather goods, precious stones etc., would definitely confuse a customer.

Brand names are pervasive throughout the market and offer cues to the consumer that can aid in his decision-process. In effect, brand names can become decision rules within the consumer's choice process. Branded goods are supposed to exhibit a certain consistency in quality, quantity and performance. For instance, Ponds India Ltd. has effectively encashed its goodwill on brand name by introducing some premium soaps in the market. Where these characteristics are maintained, brand names enable the consumers to recognize goods, and to compare them with other known brands. Thus, the consumer can formulate his own notion of expected satisfaction. Through repeated usage, the consumer learns which brand to choose and which ones to avoid.

The experience with branded goods can carry over to other product classes of some brands as well as to branded goods in general.

Linder relates brands to advertising "... as a means of making factual knowledge more accessible than otherwise ... to provide quasi information for people who lack the time to acquire the genuine insights. They get the surrogate information they want to have, in order to feel they are making the right decision[71].

He then concludes, "...Increasing reliance will be placed on "hidden persuaders" which are what consumers need to make quick decisions...brand loyalty must be built up among people who have no possibility of deciding how to act on objective grounds. As routine purchasing procedures gain in importance as a means of reducing decision making time, it will be increasingly important to capture those who have not yet developed their routines[72].

In this view, brand names become rules by which consumer can make routine decisions and thus reduce decision time. Widespread cognition of brand names is largely achieved through advertising.

Through inspection and comparison of quality and price in more stores, the consumer can acquire an overview of the market offering. Comparative shopping is limited only by the consumer's own willingness and ability to invest time and effort, relative to the increased expected satisfaction to be derived from such activities.[73] Also, the consumer can consult salesman at the retail establishment.

Salesmen at the retail establishment play an important role in high-involvement decision situations. People are used to seek advice from druggists on many aspects of health and drugs usage. In a study conducted by Claxton and Anderson, it was revealed that the new energy-use labelling programmers for major applications was found to be of little importance compared with the inputs of sales persons [74] whether or not personal selling will have much impact comes from the nature of customer-salesman interaction. It may be interesting to note that a highly dependent consumer tends to be susceptible and hence prefers assistance by a sales person in decision-making, whereas, an independent person prefers a minimum of suggestion and assistance. [75]The independent person, in fact, seems to respond more positively in aggressive selling.[76]

As a source of objective information, retailer's advice cannot always be accepted neutrally and without prejudice, since the retailer is basically interested in selling. For example, overselling is a common practice among many retailers. Also with scores of new products, the retailer may lack precise knowledge and to the extent that this assumption is correct, he can no longer give reliable product information. Further, the advent of the supermarket, discounter, and other mass merchandise has greatly reduced this source of information due to the concomitant loss of personal relationship between the retailer and his customer.

The price of the product is also a most frequently used indicator for better quality and performance expectation and many purchase decisions are based on price consideration. The consumer's syndrome that associates high quality and performance, which exist in the multitude of brands and products, price comparison as an information source can be difficult at best, misleading at worst. But Linder points out that "actual fact, it may be a very reasonable rule of thumb to equate price with quality." The mistakes made in this way may very well be less expensive than the efforts that would be required to avoid them by acquiring better information.[77]

With the emergence and widespread acceptance of major newspapers, magazines, radio and television, the mass media have become one of the most ubiquitous and inescapable facts of a society. The mass media represent a powerful force, influencing and shaping the values, tastes and quality of life. Mass media can also be viewed more as reflecting the culture than as shaping it. To marketers, mass media provide the vehicle for advertising. Advertising is an essential ingredient in almost every marketing mix, represents a principal means for making products known to potential buyers, for keeping consumers informed and for persuading many consumers to buy.

Advertising and promotion constitute one of the most important and pervasive sources of information in the market place. From the manufacturer and retailer's view, the primary objective of advertising and promotion is the selling function. From the consumer's view, advertising and promotion serves the very useful function of acquainting and promotion serves the very useful function of acquainting him with the market review of what products and brands are available, what their prices are and where and when they can be purchased. The consumer's use of print media is for the most part, selective. A reader can pass through a newspaper or a magazine, glancing at editorial material and advertising, skipping that which is of little interest and concentrating on what is deemed important.

Electronic media are more intrusive. The viewer cannot skip the commercial and go on to the programmer and so he is exposed to many commercials whether he wants or not. But the messages delivered by print media have a certain degree of permanence. To consumers who want to make decisions based on careful examinations of detailed information, advertising broadcast over the airwaves is apt to be unsatisfactory. If any important decision is to be made-especially an important decision that is over an extended period of time, the consumers can collect advertisement from different magazines or different newspapers and make comparisons among them.

The relative permanence of printed advertisements makes the consumers for repeat and "pass long" leadership. But the degree of repeat and pass long readership is much more difficult to measure and as a consequence, the aspect of print media advertising's influence is often ignored even though it may be very important.

Another difference between print and electronic media is that electronic media make it easy to appeal directly to children. Starting at about age two, children begin to pay some attention to television commercials and by the time they grow, they have already acquired a large amount of information about products they find interesting.

This information has two effects. The most direct and obvious effect is that it encourages children to ask their parents to buy special products especially toys and food items. Another subtle effect of exposure to television advertising is that it associates the brand name with a variety of appealing characters and pleasant experience.

In addition to its announcement, display and need arousal functions, advertisement serves to keep the brand name towards the front of the consumer's mind. Whether or not the advertisement can furnish a convincing demonstration or an attractive display, whether or not it can arouse and otherwise latent need, the repeated calling of the brand name to the consumers attention, gives the brand an advantage over an unknown brand when a choice must be made.

Primitive awareness must be an important function of advertising, especially advertising of established brands. So a major function of advertising must be to keep the brand name salient in the consumer's mind in spite of the consumer's tendency to forget and in the face of a continuous onslaught of competing messages.

As regards product, specific consumer information advertising has limitations. Advertising tends to take advantage of human weakness. To that extent in which this type of commercial communication is based on persuasion, image and emotion rather than on 'objective' product information per se. For example, product disadvantages are seldom revealed, thus rendering performance comparisons all but impossible on the basis of advertising alone, and comparative advertising does not alleviate this difficulty.

Consumer-Oriented Information

Included in the category of consumer-oriented sources, are all those types of information that have been designed for the express purpose of aiding the consumer in his decision making, by providing clues, facts, evolutions and comparisons of a multitude of products that are not normally available either through commercial or personal channels of communications. Since the information sources that belong to this group are normally outside commercial and personal channels, sphere, they have been called as "Independently organized consumer information system." These independent sources can be divided into three types of consumer information- quality marking, informative labelling and comparative product testing.[78]

Quality marking and informative labelling are closely related with each other insofar as both are based on some tests, which must meet criteria as specified by the issuing agency. Quality marking corresponds to a seal of approval or a quality certification, which is issued to any applicant whose products meet minimum standards of quality as established by the testing organization. Informative labels are factual descriptions of product characteristics, which indicate the grading of the product according to its performance, material, contents, size and similar factors. Often, these labels contain also instruction for proper use. The quality seal or the informative label, as the case may be, is attached to the product itself and it is common to find both quality marking and informative labels combined on the same certification.

Product testing services provide comparative information on quality characteristics, performance, usage and technical aspects of a great variety of products. Often, product rating and price comparisons are included in the test reports. Product test reports can render a valuable service by helping consumers and by stimulating quality improvements.

One author summed up his feeling about product testing in this way: "to the extent that reliable guidance is offered, the rating agencies make useful contribution to the smoother functioning of the economic system. Inaccurate information, whether disseminated by rating agencies or by advertisers tends to subvert the economy.[79]

It is probably true that the information value that can be derived from product test reports is superior in most cases to trial and error and additionally, they may help instill quality consciousness, in consumers and producers. Some limitations to product tests can be noted, however. For instance, only branded goods are feasible for testing to allow people to identify the product tested. The test sample of individual brands is typically small. Variation in quality from time to time may inhibit test validity. Tests may become obsolete too soon in a dynamic economy. Then, there is the problem of non-typical consumer whose varying product use conditions may make test results inappropriate for him. Finally, the quality characteristics of the product itself may be conflicting, such as power versus economy in a car, or toughness versus absorption capacity in a paper napkin.[80]

INFORMATION SEARCH

There are a great number and variety of sources of consumer information available to consumers with which he could sort out those clues that are relevant to a particular purchase decision to permit him to take a 'rational ' and 'optimal' choice.

The consumer is human and he is faced with limited capacities of time, money and effort. Often he must be satisfied with less than perfect information and less than optimal choice. Consumers vary in types and number of the nature of sources of information they consult, when they need information for reaching a purchase decision. Because of the nature of information sources, consumers seldom find it necessary to consult the mass media after personal sources have been consulted and they often find it necessary to supplement mass media information with information from sources they consider more complete or more truth-worthy. Variation in information search also depends on consumer's abilities to seek and use information and their perceptions of the need for pre-purchase information.

It has been assumed that consumers take in all information to which they are exposed but the significance of this assumption is not obvious. If consumers simply passively accepted all information that they accidentally encounter, they would probably die of starvation because they would be unable to carry out the act of purchasing. They would be lost in information. Therefore, this assumption must be abandoned. First, consumers are and must be very selective as regards the information they take in, because they are confronted with massive amounts of information, most of it irrelevant. Second, consumers must be tightly adaptive to changing information needs and changes in environment. At one moment, a consumer is buying chewing gum, at the next, buying an automobile. The difference in information requirements is almost astronomical. Also, the environment is continuously changing with respect to the information that it provides. Often, almost no effort is required to process the information; that is especially true of advertising. Consumers get information from their surroundings, their environment and this environment is very complex. In fact, it is probably the complexity of environment, rather than the complexity of the buyer, that makes understanding consumer behaviour so difficult.

Consumer and His Environment

A man, viewed as a behaving system, is quite simple. The apparent complexity of his behaviour over time is largely a reflection of the complexity of the environment in which he finds himself[81] Consider the enormous number of sources of information that a consumer could use for almost any product in the technologically advanced culture of post-industrial society. For example, suppose one is interested in buying a television set. He can discuss it with friends or relatives or neighbours. He can read the newspaper advertisement. He can enquire at many stores. He can watch television. He can read some of the magazines and newspapers which run articles on various products, especially when there are significant product changes.

Because of the complexity of the environment, what buyers pay attention to in the environment and where they search in that environment make a great difference to their purchasing behaviour.

This fact has two implications: first, one must attempt to understand the process of attention and search. The remarkable capacity of human -beings for selective attention and search is especially pertinent to understanding the effects of mass media, which offer a wide scope for selectivity to operate. Second, because of the environmental differences among consumers, one should not be surprised at the greater amount of variability–'noise'–that is encountered when the data is analyzed.

The consumers' environment is the source of information to which they might be exposed. An exposure situation occurs when the consumer is faced with marketing communications. The major elements of the theory of marketing communications are as follows :

Fig. 2.1 : Elements of Marketing Communications[82]

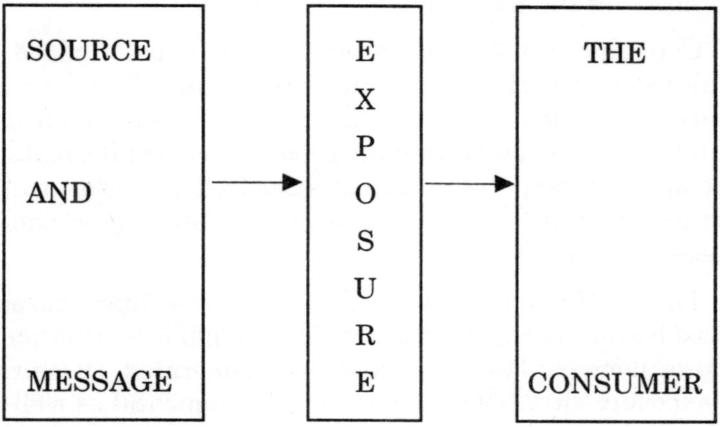

To explain the effects of communications, it is necessary to know, how and when exposure occurs (i.e, attention is paid) and to analyse what happens when the consumer pays attention to the information. Exposure may take place in three different ways, which may be (a) by way of experience formation, (b) forced learning and (c) information acquisition[83]. Experience formation is especially important in connection with the use of the products and services. Whenever consumption occurs, it is possible that the product involved will perform above or below expectations. In both instances arousal will increase and a conflict will result. In the process of dealing with the conflict perceived instrumentalities or values can change.

In forced learning situations, the information itself will generate a sufficient amount of arousal. This is what happens when advertising influence the individual when he is not actively looking for information. Only to the extent that the advertisement is able to generate a minimum of conflict, modification of concepts occurs. Information acquisition occurs when arousal has already been generated and a certain number of concepts are salient. The consumer is actively seeking out information and the information to which he will attend depends upon the salient cognitive structure, the important thing being that the initiative is in the hands of the receiver.

Consumer's information acquisition is not limited to exploration in the pre-choice situation. Choosing an alternative that implies that the consumer will go out and search for more may terminate a choice process information. But again, when the information search is performed, a certain amount of conflict is aroused, and a new choice process is generated.

The distinction between information acquisition and forced learning suggests that either individual or situational factors alone explain how exposure is generated. Of course, all exposure situations depend on environmental as well as individual factors, but the relative importance of these factors varies. On the one hand, when a firm commitment to search for some specific information has been made and when the consumer subsequently addresses himself to that information, the importance of the internal factor is obvious and the instance can easily be identified as information acquisition. On the other hand, when no intension exists and when external information makes the consumer consider a product he would not otherwise have considered, a clear case of forced learning occurs. However, often vague intensions or motivational sets interact with favourable situational elements to create the exposure. It may be more questionable whether forced learning or information acquisition occur, the essence being, of course, that forced learning and information acquisition represent extremes on a scale ranging from exposure situations in which situational factors dominate, to situations in which internal factor are the major determinants of choice.

Availability and Choice of Information

When studying situations in which the consumer is exposed to information, it is necessary to consider the availability of different kinds of information.

Consumers can be exposed to many different kinds of information, but for the individual consumer, the narrow environment in which he lives limit the information he will face. The forced learning situations he will experience are biased to the extent the environment is biased, and the same applies to the information to which he can attend in situations where he is actively acquiring information. Similarly, the consumer is not likely to have experience with all possible products and brands.

The environment may also affect in a more narrow sense which information sources the consumer will utilize. The alternatives to be considered depend upon the particular situation, and each situation has its own sources upon which the consumer must rely. Normally, if one wants to make use of other sources, he must choose an alternative that involves search outside the particular environment and such an alternative will be chosen only when a certain amount of perceived conflict has been aroused, and when no other sufficiently attractive alternatives are available.

How the consumer will react to the information depends upon the relationship between the source and content of the message and the receiver's salient cognitive structure. A particular piece of information is chosen according to the individual's expectations with regard to that information. However, when the consumer becomes exposed to the message, it may look completely different or it may turn out to be more or less in agreement with his expectations. This implies that the consumer's choice of information must be examined, depending on his expectations and that the effects of the information must be seen in relation to actual content of the information.

Selectivity implies that people are biased in the material to which they become exposed and to which they attend, in what they read and understand, and in what they learn and remember, many studies of selectivity suggests that two kinds of selectivity occur. Many authors suggest that consumers are selective in that they seek out what they are interested in; while others suggest that people prefer information that supports whatever views they already hold. In some instances, these principles may make some predictions, as when the supportive information happens to be the information in which the consumer is also interested.

Regarding the consumers interest in pre-purchase information, Thorelli (1971) [84] , in his study on 93 Norway sample districts, found that those with more education might be more information-minded than those with less education. Actual or potential buyers or owners of a product were more likely to be better informed than others, and one might expect that higher income or wealth was accompanied by greater product-informedness. There might be a product-informed elite, and hence a concentration of information power among consumers. After all knowledge is power.

In their scholarly study, Newmann and Staelin (1972)[85] ,made the findings that lend support to the hypothesis that purchase and a product resulted in learning, which later influences buyer behaviour, their results, as well as those of earlier studies indicated that the amount of information sought by many buyers was small, but it did not necessarily mean that buyers were ill-informed.

In another useful study, Rao (1972)[86] examined the relationship between the amount of explicit information and brand perceptions and the effect on perceptions of brand image (conjured up by the brand name alone) though other sources of information use were available. Twelve brands of 1970 automobile models (cars) were chosen as stimuli in the study. Description of the twelve stimuli was developed from literature published by the manufacturers and consumer union reports.

In their revealing attempts, Roering and Block (1976)[87] surveyed the following predictions as the focus of their investigation. The consumers living in high and low density areas will differ with respect to their pattern of pre-purchase information search, and consumers generally would differ with respect to the pattern of pre-purchase information search associated with the decision to buy various types of products. The data used for the above study were collected via structured personal interviews with 102 household representatives in the central Missouri area in and around the city of Columbia.

The main result of the study was that the two consumer groups studied did differ with respect to pattern of information search.

The pronounced variations in information search patterns observed in these two consumer groups suggested that other consumer groups might also show substantially different information search. Thus, this research effort had attempted to enhance understanding of pre-purchase information search by comparing the reported information search pattern of two market segments.

O'Brien (1977)[88] examined, in his study, four factors-demographic, personality, source and message and product class and their effects on information handling. The products chosen for the study were cars and breakfast. It was found that the factors had varying effects on information handling. Search initiation had no effect on these variables, nor did education, sex, product class or psychosocial classification, except that knowledge increased more for cars than instant breakfast. As demographic variables, sex and education affected search initiation. Higher educated subjects were more likely to go in search of information probably because they were more familiar with sources and benefits of such search. Males were more likely to go in such a search in difference being greater for the presumably higher interest product class of automobiles. The psychological variable, a personality measure has no effects no search or decision making but was found to influence the way information was asked.

Another important finding of the study was that since most available information was favorable towards a particular brand, unfavourable messages would be especially valuable in that damaging information could terminate purchase consideration.

In his study of choice process and automatic responses, Wasson (1979)[89] found that the general focus of consumer behaviour models on the search process seemed to have relegated the complex of automatic responses and unconsidered choices to purchase behaviour of established products. By the automatic responses was meant the learned complex of habitual procedures, of those habits of thought called perceptions and habits designed as attitudes, social class behaviour, culture and life style. The automatic responses played a major role in the adoption and diffusion of innovative new offerings, and were the determining factor in the degree of ready acceptance of the product on introduction.

In a fine and fruitful attempt, Westbrook (1979)[90] made a study to determine whether distinctive patterns of information source usage could be identified. A method based on canonical analysis of retail, neutral and personal sources usage measures in connection with selected explanatory variables proved useful distinguishing four different patterns. The products chosen for the study were refrigerators, freezers, washing machines, clothes dryers, ovens, and dishwashers.

The findings of the study indicated that major appliance buyers could be classified according to distinctive patterns of pre-purchase information source usage, which were understandable in terms of various explanatory variables.

Yet another commendable study was made by Crites, Shaw and Onkvisit (1979)[91] on information sources usage among home buying consumers. The main purposes of the study were: what exactly the steps involved in the home search process? And what were the types of information sources used by consumers to locate potential homes for purchase consideration? A field study was organized to examine the information search patterns of purchase and post-purchase home buying sample consumers of 2,314 was determined out of the population of 18,517.

There were five classifications on the level of interest with regard to the purchase of a home – slightly involved, involved, very actively involved, post-purchase, and not involved. The findings of the study indicated that for most Americans the purchase of a home represents the single largest purchase a family would make in its lifetime. The data gathered in this study indicated that changes did occur during the search process and it might be of interest to determine how the changes occurred and what influenced the consumer to change the search pattern.

A model was developed by Ratchford (1980)[92], expressing the relation between gains to search and a consumer's reference function. For four of five appliance – air-conditioner, refrigerator, washing machine, canister vacuum and range – to which the model was applied, extensive search would not be worthwhile for a consumer whose preference approximates the market hedonic price function. He had made a reference of other studies (Claxton Fry and Portis, 1974, Newmann and Staelin, 1972), which suggested that substantial number of consumers failed to engage in extensive search prior to purchase. But unlike previous research, his study focused on incentives for information seeking for a given product, how much would a utility-maximising consumer with a given preference gain from search.

Another informative study was undertaken on information seekers and information system by Thorelli and Engledow (1980)[93]. Consumer information systems in general and independent consumer information programmer in particular were seen as indispensable elements of consumer policy, both private and public. In open market democracies, information had inherent merit relative to consumer protection by direct regulation.

In a comprehensive study of the behaviours and correlates of information seeking by Australian new car buyers, the researcher Keil and Layton (1981)[94] examined three dimensions of information seeking–a source of information dimension, a brand dimension, and a time dimension. Cluster analysis was used to develop consumer taxonomies of search behaviour based on measurements of each of the dimensions. The resulting taxonomies were a high search group, a low search group, and three clusters collectively styled selective information seekers.

The findings of the above study were that the Australian consumers like their U.S counterparts, differ greatly in their use of alternative information seeking behaviour studied, the results indicated that some consumers undertook substantial activity. 36% of respondents had reported making two or few trips to inspect cars, whereas 20% reported making six or more such trips. The relationship between price and search behaviour was positive, indicating that the greater the net price paid, the longer the search time period.

In another belief-oriented survey of 164 recent purchasers of colour television sets, Buncan and Olshavsky (1982)[95] showed that consumer beliefs about the marketplace and about their capabilities as consumers accounted for 50% of the variance in extent of external search. The type of brand (domestic, foreign, or private) and the type of store (national, regional, or local) considered by a consumer were found to be significantly related to the belief held.

The main objective of this research was to study the degree of relationship between market place related beliefs and pre-purchase external information search behaviour. The extent of external search for information exhibited by consumers prior to purchase typically had been found to be very limited; in some cases little or no external search occurred.

Another enlightening study by Malhotra, Jain and Lagakos, (1982)[96] reviewed the information overload controversy and presented a methodology for investigating the effects of information load on consumer decision making process.

A comparative study of consumer information seeking between two countries-Singapore and U.S. was taken up by Tan and Dolich (1983)[97] The results of the study revealed that contrary to the belief that foreign consumers might utilize different information sources, it was found that the U.S. and Singapore respondents to be quite alike in their usage of information sources. In general, personal sources such as observing or seeking advice from friends, neighbors and family members were used quite frequently by both groups, seeking information at retail outlets appears to be common among the U.S. consumers only.

POSITION OF CONSUMER IN THE MARKET

Consumer may be defined as any person or individual who is using goods and services for the satisfaction of his needs and wants. This definition depends on usage and not on the act of purchasing per se, nor on income, age, sex, or social class. Since all persons living in the society are dependent on one another for providing the necessities of life (as well as its luxuries) and all individuals are using up, i.e. consuming, at the minimum, some food, clothes and shelter, all are included in the consumer category. Engel[98] and others defined consumption as " those acts of individuals directly involved in obtaining and using economic goods and services, including the decision process using economic that precede and determine these acts." Excluded from the concepts is state and local government's 'usage' as well as industry 'usages' for consumption and for production can be drawn because the consumer may not be under the same pressure to act rationally as is the firm of entrepreneur. The entrepreneur who behaves irrationally will presumably be driven out of business and will then no longer be a 'producer.' Even government is somewhat obliged to act rationally, - at least in the eyes of the majority or risk loss of re-election. An irrational consumer, on the other hand, even if driven to bankruptcy, cannot stop consuming unless he commits suicide.

The inclusion of the consumer in the market system is, of course, as old as the history of exchange -based economies. His role in this system as a performer of marketing activities and his strength relative to other market forces, however, have changed.

On the macro level, consumers seem to have gained in relative market position.[99] More discretionary income has enabled consumers to afford more luxuries, more travel, and more recreational activities. Increased leisure time has encouraged consumers to partake in these amenities of life in larger numbers.

Katona attributes the greater influence of modern consumers on the economy if broad masses of people were entirely uninformed about economic events.[100]

However, consumers have largely remained unorganized and unconcentrated. As a result, consumers as individuals may at times be confused by the large assortment of the marketing offer. This may be frustrated by the impersonal character and treatment by mass merchandisers. While government, industry and trade; as well as the labour unions have grown enormously, often highly centralized power structures, consumers have remained largely diffused.

FACTORS INFLUENCING THE CONSUMER IN THE DECISION MAKING PROCESS:

After the consumer has decided the criteria to be considered, he evaluates various alternatives, and then makes a choice between different products. In this process, he is influenced by motivation.

"Motivation can be described as the driving force within individuals that impels them to action".[101] Successful marketers define their markets in terms of the needs of the consumers they are trying to satisfy, rather than products they sell. This need appears to be closely related to the ego need, in that many individuals experience increased self-enhancement when they exercise power over objects or people. A number of products lend themselves to promises of power superiority for users, and durable goods are the best example for it.

A significant research work was carried out by Peters (1970) [102] who introduced a study on the combination of family's income and occupation as a new explanatory variable, but earlier studies focused either income or occupation alone. He chose a representative sample of 2453 families, which consisted of those that had recent model cars and those that did not have five classes of car compact, intermediate-sized, medium-sized, large and foreign economy-cars were selected for the study.

The above study revealed that the average income-class, regardless of occupation, own foreign economy, and intermediate-sized and compact cars than expected. Moreover, the over privileged group (regardless of occupation) owned more medium-sized and large cars.

The concept of social class in marketing was introduced in 1950. A noteworthy study by Myres, Stanton and Hong (1971)[103] compared social class and income as correlations of buying behaviour for a variety of low-cost packaged goods. The objective of this study was to determine whether social class or income best explains which products are found in homes. One thousand households were selected by multi-stage area probability sample. The social class was found basically inferior to income as a correlate of buying behaviour for the consumer packaged goods covered in their study.

What goes on in the minds of a consumer as he forms a purchase decision was marvelously studied by O'Brien (1971)[104] in his novel study on consumer decision making. He used a relatively new methodology with a computer for setting up and interpreting multiple time-period survey data. The significant cross-legged and multiple correlation differences indicate that word-of-mouth influenced subsequent intention to purchase. Further, it was significant to note that commercial information has no direct influence on ultimate purchase. O'Brien's research is a revealing one indeed.

Settle (1972)[105] made a study, examining consumers' preferences for four kinds of information sources in order to subjectively validate attribution about four types of products. Totally 24 products were chosen for the study like stereos, chairs, watches, bracelets, cookware's, electric hair rollers, oven-toasters, electric blenders, etc.

The study attempted to classify products so that conditions of purchase and use would be similar within classes. The conditions related not so much to the physical or economic properties of the product as to the psychological properties and the motivation of the potential buyers.

Another study was conducted by Lambert (1972)[106] to test whether behavioural differences existed among consumers who selected items priced differently within the same product. The products chosen for the study were tape recorders, portable stereos, molded luggage, tooth paste, coffee, suntan lotion, and tennis rackets. The findings revealed that persons who chose the high-priced items perceived large quality variation within the product category and saw the consequences of a poor choice as being undesirable. They were confident that quality was related to price and saw themselves as good judges of product quality. Their perceived experience in purchasing the product was often high and they thought brand choice was likely to affect other people's social judgement of them.

Bogart and Lehman (1973)[107] ,in their psychological study of unaided brand, recall by female household heads, examined some factors related to brand salience. Their findings indicated that brand recall was a complex and dynamic process.

Newmann and Werbel (1974)[108] were much interested in some new findings on automobile brand loyalty. Though brand loyalty is a subject of high interest to marketers, the empirical research on it has been limited especially to consumer durables. A new measure of loyalty was compared with the traditional repurchase definition, and significant influences on loyalty were identified by multivariate analysis.

The data analysed for the above study were from 217 households, which had bought a new car in 1967 or 1968. The respondents were adults from a probability sample of 1300 households in the United States, excluding Alaska. The findings revealed that the probability of loyalty was higher than average for persons who attended but did not graduate from either high school or college who were in occupations of low to medium skills who bought cars frequently; who tender to be optimistic and who were satisfied with their cars. A remarkable study was made by Parker and Copley (1974)[109] to examine the relationship which existed between consumer brand preference, attitudes, brand attributes importance and perception. The data were collected from the twin cities of Lewiston, Idali and Clarkston, and Washington. Information on preferences towards seven car brands, perceptions of the attributes of these cars and attribute satisfaction scores were obtained from the sample consumers. Eleven-car attributes-economy of operation, power, warranty, style, size and dependability-were included in the analysis.

The findings of the above research work revealed that brand evaluation was a comparative process in which the preference of one brand was highly dependent upon the consumer's attribute perceptions and attitudes toward other brands.

A comparative study on qualitative and quantitative models was made on brand loyalty by Wheeler (1974)[110] which threw light on many behavioural aspects like brand-switching. Consumer behaviour was more accurately predicted by means of quantitative models than qualitative ones. The study also emphasized and quantitative taxes because a brand loyal customer purchases a particular brand not only time and again but the brand under consideration have positive psychological preferences also for the brand loyal customer.

Fear can also be an important factor of motivation. In this regard, a study was undertaken by Tesar, (1974)[111] in the case of electric car, the need for which was felt by citizens of America due to the fear of air pollution. Metropolitan areas were the hardest hit. The people were forced to change their attitudes due to a change in the environment. The electric car is pollution-free and does not require petro-chemically-based fuel. In speaking to the third International Electric Vehicle Symposium, James A. Meclore, United States Senator from Idaho, expressed the opinion that the electric car was one of the few realistic solutions to the transportation problems.

The above survey was conducted to test the consumer reactions to the product concept, which included 1200 personal interviews at the shopping centers in three large metropolitan statistical areas in the Midwest in the latter part of spring, 1973. The hypothesis framed made it easy to test the intention of buying with different attributes cost of operation, ease of maintenance, luggage capacity, passenger capacity, mileage, price, speed and pollution. The researchers forecast a definite increase in sales upto 2,46,000 electric cars by 1980.

Parker and Anderson (1974)[112] examined the consumer's preferential expectations concerning attributes on objects and their postrial perceptions of the attributes. The findings suggested that differences did exist among individuals in terms of the appropriateness of various preference models.

Hempel (1975)[113] studied terminates and effects of family role structures in house purchasing decision. A sample of 206 households was selected and both husbands and wives were interviewed. The findings of the study revealed that the role structure in family house buying decisions was affected by household characteristics. There was variation in the relative importance of determinants. There was variation in the relative importance of determinants across sex, culture and role structure measure.

A useful attempt was made by Wood Side (1975)[114] to examine as to who makes the purchase of automobiles from information on marital roles in prior stages in the decision-making processes and from demographic and psychographic data. The data were obtained from a cross-sectional survey of 200 families from three housing sub divisions in the Columbia, South Carolina, metropolitan area, in 1972. Husbands and wives were interviewed that some of the developing family types did exist through the analysis of relative influence in prior decision-making and demographic-psychographic data.

The problems of methodology encountered in data collections in choice of participants and in decision-making concepts were analyzed and studied by Dunsing and Haftstrom (1975).[115]

A significant culture study was made by Henry (1976)[116] to support the general theory that culture was a determinant of certain aspects of consumer behaviour. Value dimensions developed to study the cultural orientations within American society were found to correlate with the ownership of generic automobiles categories. Culture generally is accepted by marketing theorists as one of the underlying determinants of consumer behaviour.

The psychological implication in the consumer behaviour, when a change of agency is effected was brilliantly studied by Nordstrom (1976) [117] who had assumed that changes in market structure variables could affect consumer loyalty behaviour. This research work presented supportive evidence from an expo facto experiment showing that a change in business ownership was related to significantly altered brand and store loyalty patterns. It made a reference to Ford agency. These findings highlighted a need to recognize that loyalty was dependent on factors outside the physical product as motivation and that to hold loyal the buyers, from the viewpoint of dealers, there must be continuity of operation.

In another in-depth study, by Paul and Rayn (1976)[118] perceived risk at the brand level was investigated. Perceived risk was conceptualized in terms of expected negative utility associated with automobile brand preferences. Empirical evidence supported the notion that importance of loss was more useful as a segmentation variable than as a component in a multiplicative model.

A study was undertaken by Tankersley (1977)[119] with the objectives to investigate the association between attitude and brand loyalty behaviour to compare two attitude models' association to brand loyalty behaviour and to analyze the effects of intervening variables on the association between attitude and brand behaviour. This study threw light on the relationship that existed between attitude and brand loyal behaviour.

Whether customers behave rationally or irrationally while taking buying decisions was a unique study made by Markin (1979).[120] The study examined several aspects including the typical models and assumptions inherent in consumer decision process models and to develop the psychological concept of rationalization and examine the existential support for the concept. The findings revealed that the consumers were sometimes rational and not always. Consumers did rationalize their decisions and the rational consumer obsessed with seeking, searching and information processing activity was largely a normative rather than a positive model.

Golden (1979)[121] in his relative study, investigated the influence of comparative and non-comparative advertising on purchase intention ratings, perceptions of believability, credibility, quantity of information, and usefulness of information. The impact of the advertisers' competitive position and claim was considered.

In order to measure certain concepts–self concept, reason concepts and product concepts–Malhotra (1981)[122] had made a study regarding construction of a scale to measure the above concepts. Multi-variate analysis and multi-dimensional scaling procedures were employed to develop a 15-item semantic differential scale measures of test-retest reliability were reported.

A remarkable study on family decision making was undertaken by Qualls (1981).[123] The main purpose of the research was to discover the effects of family members' sex-role orientation on influence patterns for several household decisions. The comparison of sex-role modern and sex-role traditional revealed that family members' sex-role orientation affects the degree to which families interact and the perceived pattern of influence for various family decisions.

A study of quality was made by Rexeisen (1981)[124] to scrutinize the influence of price on products evaluations. The result of the study was quite contrary to earlier studies that no significant price effects were found. There were significant interactions between place of purchase, information levels and the ordering of price presentation.

Freuden and Bible (1982)[125] made a status to examine whether tenure status and socio-economic status were associated with housing attribute preference. One hundred and fifty five homeowners were selected as sample. The findings revealed that tenure status and socioeconomic characteristics affected the housing choice.

A consumer involvement study was undertaken by Laurent and Kapferer (1985).[126] The researchers measured an involvement profile rather than a single involvement level. Fourteen product categories – durables, food, textiles, drugs, etc., - were selected for the study, with 100 housewives as a sample. It was found that when consumers were involved, they engaged in a number of behaviour (active search, extensive choice process, active information processing, etc.,) and when not involved, they were not engaged in these behaviours.

Analysis study was conducted by Bitta, Monrose and McGinnis (1986)[127] who dealt with the issue of comparative price advertising from a behaviour perspective.

The study by Srinivasan (1979)[128] examined two aspects, cognitive-rational and hedonist aspects, as forming two distinct but consecutive stages of the consumer process. The findings revealed that cognitive-rational and hedonist aspects were not two mutually exclusive elements in consumers' scheme of things.

Hill (1987)[129] made a study on the mood of consumer with the objectives of looking at the mood literature and its development thereof.

Ravichandran (1988)[130],in this praiseworthy research work, examined information sources used, choice-marking and discrimination between urban and semi-urban population with reference to purchase of durable goods with 550 sample consumers from Chennai city and 4 other towns. The products chosen were refrigerators, televisions, ceiling fans and domestic mixers. The fruitful findings revealed that urban consumers made use of commercial sources, and semi-urban, personal sources. They showed significant differences in the time taken for decision.

AN OVERVIEW OF EVALUATION CRITERIA PROCESS

Economic and market analyses attempt to identify and describe the influences underlying market activities so that with the fuller understanding more useful predictions can be made about future trends. Since firms prosper by serving their customers' needs at a profit to themselves, some understanding of the behaviour of customers during the various stages of buying appears to be a pre-requisite to successful trading operations. Firms should therefore, construct profiles of their customers, which will include comprehensive analysis of the buying situation. This systematic situation should be based on data from market research, together with first hand knowledge of customer's behaviour gained over several years.

The decision process perspective provides important information for marketing decision making. Knowledge about such things as the relative importance of various information sources, the criteria used to evaluate alternative brands and so on, is useful in designing product, price, channel and selling strategies.

Information has been processed and is part of long-term memory. It is available for use in alternative evaluation process that consists of the comparison of various alternatives evaluation process that consists of the comparison of various alternatives for purchase and consumption against those criteria or product attributes felt by the consumers to be important in the decision. The outcome will be formation of or change in beliefs, attitudes and intentions.

OPERATIONAL DEFINITIONS

Consumer

Strictly, the ultimate consumer of a product, the ultimate user of a product or service is the person who derives the satisfaction or the benefit offered.[131]

According to the Consumer Protection Act, 1986 U/S 2(1)(d) the term 'consumer' is defined as a person who buys goods or hires any service for consideration, paid or promised and includes user of goods, using them with the approval of the buyer, but does not include a person who obtains goods for resale or for any other commercial purpose.

A consumer is an individual, who consumes goods, manufactured by firms or created by nature (air, water etc.), and services offered by government or firms, hospital, educational institutions etc.[132]

Customer

Person or organization, actually making the purchasing decisions, is not necessarily the 'consumer' or 'user'. Legally, he is a party to a contract for the sale of goods.[133]

"A customer is the most important visitor on our premises. He is not dependent on us. We are dependent on him. He is not an interruption in our work. He is the purpose of it. He is not an outsider to our business. He is a part of it. We are not doing him a favour by serving him. He is doing a favour by giving us an opportunity to do so"-Gandhiji.

Durable Goods

Goods providing a service over period of time rather than extinguished at the moment of consumption: includes goods like television, motorcars, and refrigerators.[134]

Potential Consumers

Consumers who intended to purchase durable products in the next six months from the month in which they were contacted for data collection.

User

Consumers who were using durable products at the time of data collection.

Consumer Attitudes

Consumption related attitudes of the consumer of durable products that are formed on the basis of evaluation of information, considering, advertisements, interpersonal sources, price, brand/company name, store name, perceived risk and psychographics.

Product Attributes

Those attributes that were identified in the pilot study as important to the potential buyers in selecting durable products viz., brand name and price, defrost facility and durability.

Two Types of Consumers

The term consumer is often used to describe two different kinds of consuming entities: the personal consumer and the organizational consumer, the personal consumer buys goods and services for his or her own use (e.g. shaving cream or lipstick) for the use of the household (salad dressing) for just one member of the household (a shirt) or as a gift for a friend (a book). These are personal consumers.

The second category of consumer, the organizational consumer, encompasses profit and not-for-profit businesses, government agencies (local and nationals) and institutions (schools, churches, prisons) all of which must buy products, equipments, and services in order to run their organizations, which may be operated for profit (e.g. commercial enterprises) or not-for-profit (e.g., governmental agencies, museums or hospitals).

Buyers and Users

The person who makes the actual purchase is not always the user or the only user of the product in question. Nor is the purchaser necessarily the person who makes the product decision. A mother may buy a product for her children (who are the users). Buyers are not always the users or the only users of the products; they neither buy nor are they necessarily the persons who make the product selection decision.

Consumers are highly involved in a purchase when it is expensive, bought infrequently and risky. Products involve a decision-making unit, which consists of more than a single person. Consider the selection of a family durable product. The suggestion to buy a new television might come from the oldest child (initiator). A friend might advice the family on the kind of durable products to buy (influencer). The husband might choose the make (decider). The wife might have definite desire regarding the durable products look. The husband might make the final decision, with the wife approving (buyer). The wife might end up using the durable products more than the husband does (user). A company must identify these different roles as they have implications for designing the product, determining messages, and allocating the promotional budgets.

Consumer Behaviour and Government Decision-Making

In recent years, the relevance of consumer-behaviour principles to governmental decision-making has become quite evident. Two major areas of activity have been affected: 1) Government policies that provide services to the public or result in decisions that influence consumer behviour and 2) The design of legislation to protect consumer or to assist them in evaluation of products and services.[135]

Perceived Risk

Risk or uncertainty regarding the most appropriate purchase decision or the consequences of the decision is a significant variable influencing the total amount of information gathered by consumers.

It is important to recognize that risk is subjective. That is, the risk involved in a purchase decision is perceived by the consumer and may or may not bear a strong relationship to what actually exits. For example, even the choice of a canned ram may involve considerable risk in terms of the impression a person wishes to make when purchasing it for a dinner party involving his or her boss.

Situation Influencing Risk

There are several situations that influence the consumer's perception of uncertainty or consequences.

Types of Risk

As one may expect, there are also several kinds of risk that consumer may perceive in a purchase situation.

(a) Monetary or financial risk

(b) Functional or performance risk

(c) Physical risk

(d) Social risk

(e) Psychological risk

Dealing with Risk

Because most purchase behaviour appears to involve at least some risk, consumer may take various steps to handle the problem. In most cases, this results in attempts to reduce risk. Consumer develops various strategies to relieve perceived risk.[136]

SECTION SUMMARY

As can be seen from the above discussion of personal, commercial and independent information sources, the consumer can pick his choice from a wide variety. Taken in combination, these sources of information provide the consumer with ample opportunity to gather market intelligence on a wide variety of products. Not all consumers take advantage of this opportunity. Some may lack necessary education and awareness. Others may feel the reward from information search is not worth the effort. Sometimes, communications messages are confusing rather than enlightening. His task of sorting out the relevant clues from an array of different information sources can be trying. Trust in the reliability and accuracy of individual source may also be an important factor in determining the direction and amount of search activity. The average consumer is likely to fall somewhere between the two extremes. Neither will he seek the advice of all possible information, nor will he avoid all.

For the purpose of this study, the sources of information grouped under three categories are: [a] personal sources, [b] commercial sources [including mass media] and [c] retail outlet sources. In the Indian context, the use of Engel's classification of information sources is rather untenable, for the simple reason that quality marking, information labeling and comparative product test, included in the consumer-oriented sources, are not widely practiced. With respect to the four products considered here such types of consumer information is often lacking. So, the modified groups of information sources have been used. This fact is also proved at the time of testing the draft questionnaire. Personal source includes information from friends, relatives, neighbours, past experience with the product, personal observation and examination. Commercial source includes advertisement in newspapers, magazines, books, pamphlets, consumer reports, radio, television, roadside hoardings and movie [cinema]. Retail outlet source includes information from salesmen, personal shop visits and retail outlet. Hence, it is important for a marketer to note that the above three sources of information is mostly used by the consumers in taking decision in the purchase of durable products.

In this study, the following variables are considered as evaluative criteria for taking any purchase decisions. They are price [equal and cheaper], brand popularity, availability of the product, reputation and location of the dealer, technical performance, service and availability of spare-parts, model qualities [size, colour, style etc.], warranty, discounts and gifts.

After extensive pre-information search and evaluation criteria, the consumers go for a product because of the influence of certain factors of motivation. Motivation impels the consumers to action. It is a driving force within an individual. Therefore, this chapter discusses the factors which the influence the consumers to purchase a durable products.

REFERENCES AND NOTES

1. Ira Horowitz, (1970), "Decision Making and the Theory of the Firm," Holt, Rinehart and Winston, Inc, New York, Chapter 2.
2. Frank H. Knight, (1948), "Risk Uncertainty and Profits,", Houghton Mifflin Co., New York, part-3.
3. John Von Neumann and Oskar Morgenstern, (1964), "Theory of Games and Economic Behaviour," John Wiley and Sons, Inc., New York, part 4.
4. Helmut Becker, (1971), "Consumer Information and the Image of Advertising in Germany with Significant Comparisons to America," Unpublished Ph.D. dissertation, Indiana University, p. 9.
5. George J. Stigler, (June 1961), "The Economics of Information", *Journal of Political Economy,* Vol.69, pp. 213-225.
6. George Katona and Eva Mueller, (1955), "A Study of Purchase Decisions", Lincoln H. Clerk, ed., "Consumer Behaviour", New York University , New York. p. 50.
7. Staffan B. Linder, (1970),"The Harried Leisure Class", Columbia University Press, New York , p. 69.
8. Robert Bartels, (1966), "The Development of Marketing Thought," Homewood, Richard D. Irwin, Inc., New York, p. 111.
9. Wrone Alderson, (1957), "Marketing Behaviour and Executive Action," Homewood, Richard D. Irwin, Inc., New York,. p.111.
10. John A. Howard, (1963), "Marketing Management : Analysis and Planning, Homewood," Richard D. Irwin, Inc., Chapter 3 and 4. p. 111.

11. Francesco M. Nicosia, (1966), "Consumer Decision Processes: marketing and Advertising Implications," Englewood Cliffs, N.J.: Prentice Hall, Inc. p. 21.

12. James F. Engel, David T. Kollat, and Roger D. Blackwell, (1966), "Consumer Behaviour," Holt Rinehart and Winston, Inc., New York, (3rd ed.), p. 41.

13. Ibid. p.45.

14. Robert J. Lavidge and Gary A. Steiner, (October 1961), "A Model for Predictive Measurement of Advertising Effectiveness", *Journal of Marketing,* Vol.25, pp. 59-62.

15. Brain Copland, (1963) "An Evaluation of Conceptual Frameworks for Measuring Advertising Results", in Proceedings of the Ninth Annual Conference, Advertising Foundation.

16. Kristian S. Palda, (February 1966),"The Hypothesis of a Hierarchy of Effects: A partial Evaluation", *Journal of Marketing Research,* Vol.III, p. 13.

17. Kristian S. Palda , (1964), "The Measurement of Cumulative Advertising Effects," Englewood Cliffs, N.J.: Prinetice-Hall, Inc.,

18. Philip Kotler, (1967), Marketing Management : Analysis, Planning and Control, Englewood Cliffs, N.J.: Prinetice-Hall, Inc, Chapter 18.

19. Lee k. Anderson, James R. Taylor and Robert J. Holloway, (1966),"The Consumer and His Alternatives: An Experimental Approach", *Journal of Marketing Research,* February, Vol.III, pp. 62-67.

20. Ibid. pp.73-79.

21. Stigler, op cit., pp. 232-240.

22. Anderson, op.cit., p. 67.

23. W. Edwards, (1964),"Information Seeking to Reduce the Risk of Decision", predecisional Processes in Decision Making: Proceedings of a Symposium, Ohio: Wright–patterson Air Force Abase, December, pp. 64-77.

24. Paul E. Green, Peter T. Fitzroy and Patrick J. Robinson, (1968), "Experimental Gaming in the Economics of Information", Application of the Science in Marketing Management, ed., Frank M. Bass, et.al, John Wiley and Sons, Inc., New York pp. 333-56.

25. Raymond A. Bauer, (1960), "Consumer Behaviour as Risk Taking". Dynamic Marketing for a Changing World, ed., Robert S. Hancock, Chicago, American Marketing Association, pp. 389-98.

26. Paul E. Green, (1968), "Consumer use of Information". On knowing the Consumer, ed., Joseph Newman, John Wiley and Sons, Inc New York pp. 333-56.

27. John Wilding and Raymond A. Bauer, (1968), "Consumer Goals and Reaction to a Communication Source", *Journal of Marketing Research,* February, Vol.V, pp. 73-77.

28. James F. Engel, David A. Knapp and Deanne E. Knapp, (1966), "Sources of Influence in the Acceptance of New Products for Self-Medication: preliminary Findings", Science, Technology and Marketing, Chicago, American Marketing Association, , pp. 776-82.

29. Donald J. Hempel, (1966), "An Experimental Study of the Effects of Information on Consumer Product Evaluation", Science, Technology and Marketing, ed., R.M.,Haas, Chicago, American Marketing Association, pp. 589-97.

30. Kelman H.C. and J. Cohler, (1959), "Reactions to Persuasive Communication as a Function of Cognitive Needs and Styles", Meetings of Eastern Psychological Association, Atlantic city. April, p.53.

31. George C. Katona and Eva Mueller, op.cit. p. 26.

32. Dommermuth W.P., (1965), "The Shopping Matrix and Marketing Strategy", *Journal of Marketing Research,* May, Vol.II, pp. 128-132.

33. Donald F. Cox, (1967), "Risk Handling in Consumer Behaviour: An Intensive Study of Two Cases", Donald F. Cox, ed., Risk Taking and Information Handling in Consumer Behaviour, Harvard University, p.71.

34. Joseph W. Newmann and Richard Staelin, (1973), "Information Sources of Durable Goods", *Journal of Advertising Research,* April, Vol. VI. pp. 19-29.

35. Newmann and Staelin, (1973), op.cit. p.45.

36. Raymond A. Bauer, (1963), "The Initiative of the Audience", *Journal of Advertising Research,* Vol. III, No. 2, pp. 2-7.

37. James F. Engel, et.al., op.cit. pp.776-782.

38. John A Howard and Jagdish N. Sheth, (1969), The Theory of Buyer Behaviour, John Wiley and Sons. New York, p.62.

39. Francesco M. Nicosia, op.cit., p.71.

40. Robert B.Woodruff, (1972), "Measurement of Consumers Prior Brand Information." *Journal of Marketing Research,* August, Vol.IX, pp. 258-263.

41. Ibid. p. 258-263.

42. John D. Claxton, Joseph N. Fry and Bernard Portis, (1974), "A Taxonomy of pre-purchase Information Gathering Patterns", *Journal of Consumer Research,* December, Vol. I, pp. 35-42.

43. George Katona, and Eva Mueller, op.cit. p.72.

44. Joseph N. Newmann and Richard Staelin, (1971), "Multivariate Analysis of Differences in Buyer Decision Time", *Journal of Marketing Research,* May, Vol.8, pp. 192-98.

45. Joseph N. Newmann and Richard Staelin, (1972), "Prepurchase Information Seeking for New Cars and Major Household Applications", *Journal of Marketing Research,* August, Vol.9. pp. 249-57.

46. Robert A. Westbrook, and Claes Fornel,·(1979), "Patterns of Information Source Usage Among Durable Goods Buyers", *Journal of Marketing Research,* August, Vol XVI, pp.303-12.

47. Newmann and Staelin, (1972,1973), op.cit. p. 23.

48. Claxton, et.al., (1974), op.cit. p.91.

49. Newmann and Staelin, (1973), op.cit. p. 52.

50. Claxton, et al, (1974), op.cit. p.81.

51. James F.Engel and M.Lawrence Light, (1968), "The Role of Psychological Commitment in Consumer Behaviour'" Applications of the Science, in Marketing Management,ed., Frank M.Bass, et.al., John Wiley and sons, Inc. New York, pp.179-206.

52. Paul E. Green, op. cit., p. 80.

53. James F. Engel et. Al., (1968), op.cit., pp.388-500.

54. John. A. Howard, Marketing Management, Homewood, III:, Richard D. Irwin, Inc., (1963), Chapters 3 and 4.

55. James F. Engel and Roger D. Blackwell, (1987), "Consumer Behaviour", Holt-Saunders International Edition, p. 355.

56. John. R. Kerr and Bruce Weale, (1970), "Collegiate Clothing Purchasing Patterns and Fashion Adoption Behaviour, Southern *Journal of Business,* July, pp. 91-98.

57. John Arndt, (1967) "Role of Product-Related Conversation in the Diffusion of a New product", *Journal of Marketing Research,* August, pp. 291-95.

58. George Katona and Eva Mueller, (1955), "A study of Purchasing Decisions", in Lincoln H. Clerk ed., Consumer Behaviour: The Dynamics of Consumer Reaction, New York University Press, New York, p. 45.

59. Roger D. Blackwell and W. Wayne Talarzyk, (1977), Consumer Attitude Toward Health Care and Malpractice, Columbus, Grid Publishing, Inc. p. 20.

60. Elihu Katz and Paul F. Lazarsfeld, (1955), Personal Influence, The Free Press, New York, p. 12.

61. Charles W. King, (1963),"Fashion Adoption: A Robuttal to the Trickle Down Theory", Stephen A. Greyse ed., Towards Scientific Marketing, American Marketing Association, Chicago, pp. 108-125.

62. Alvin J. Silk, (1966), "Overlap Among Self Designated Opinion Leaders : A study of Selected Dental Products and Services", *Journal of Marketing Research,* (August), pp. 255-59.

63. Elihu Katz, (1958), "Social Itinerary of Technical Changes Two Studies in diffusion of Innovation", human Organisation, 1961, pp. 70-82; E.M. Rogers and G.M. Beal, "The Importance of Personal Influence in the Adoption of Technological Changes, "Social Forces, May, pp. 329-335.

64. James Coleman, Elihu Katz and Herbert Menzel, (1957),"The Diffusion of an Innovation among Physicians", Sociometry, December, pp. 253-70; Herbert Menzel and Elihu Katz, (1955-56), "Social Relations and Innovation in the Medical Profession: The Epidemiology of a New Drug", Public Opinion Quaterly, Winter, pp. 337-52.

65. George M. Beal and Everett M. Rogers, (1957),"International Source in the Adoption Process of New Fabrie", *Journal of Home Economics,* (October), pp. 630-34.

66. John Arndt, Word-of-Month Advertising and Perceived Risk, (1968), "Prospectives in Consumer Behaviour", ed., *Harold H. Kassarjian and Thomas B. Robertson,* Glenview III., scott, Foreman and Company, pp. 330-336.

67. Everett M. Rogers, (1962), Diffusing of Innovations, The Free Press, New York pp.238 and 239.

68. Everett M. Rogers and Floyd Shoemaker, (1972), Communications Innovations: Across Cultural Approach, the Free Press, New York, p.136.

69. Fred D. Reynolds and William D. Wells, (1977), Consumer Behaviour, McGraw-Hill p. 275.

70. John Arndt, (1967), "Word-of-Month Advertising", , Advertising Research Foundation, New York, Fred D. Reynolds and Williams R. Darden, (1971),"Mutually Adaptive Effects of Inter-Personal Communications", *Journal of Marketing Research,* November ,Vol.8 , pp. 449-54.

71. Staffan B. Linder, (1970), The Harried Leisure Class, Columbia University Press, New York, p. 71.

72. Ibid, p. 71.

73. Anthony Downs, (1961),"A theory of Consumer Efficiency," *Journal of Retailing,* Vol. 37, pp 6-12,50-51.

74. John D.Claxton and C.Dennis Anderson, (1976), "Energy Information at the Point of Sale : A field Experiment," Olson Advances, pp.277-82.

75. M. Zockerman and H.J.Grosz, (1950), "Suggestability and Dependency," *Journal of Consulting Psychology*, October, Vol. 26, pp. 32-38.

76. James E. Stafford and Thomas Y.Greer, (1965), "Consumer Preference for Types of Salesmen : A Study of Independence-Dependence Characteristics, Journal of Retailing, Summer, pp. 27-33.

77. Linder, op. cit., p.69.

78. Hans B. Thorelli, (1965),"The Test Makers-A Non-Comparative Study of Organized Consumer Information in Europe", Marketing and Economic Development, ed., Peter O.Bennet, , American marketing Association, Chicago, pp. 51.71.

79. Eugene R.Beem, (1952),"Consumer Financed Testing and Rating Agencies," *Journal of Marketing*, (January), p. 272.

80. Eugene R.Beem, op. cit, p. 272.

81. H.A. Simon, (1969), The Science of Artificial, M.I.T. Press, Cambridge, Mass., p. 52.

82. Flemming Hansen, (1972), "Consumer Choice Behaviour : A Cognitive Theory," The Free Press, New York, p.164.

83. Flemming Hansen, op.cit., p.168.

84. Hans B. Thorelli, (1971), "Concentration of Inforjation Power Among Consumers." *Journal of Marketing Research,* November, Vol.8 (4), pp. 427-438.

85. Joseph W.Newman and Richard Staelin, (1972), "Pre-purchase Information Seeking for New Cars and Motor Household Appliances". *Journal of Marketing Research,* August, Vol. IX , pp. 249-257.

86. Vithala R. Rao, (1972), "Changes in Explicit Informaiton and Brand percepotions". *Journal of Marketing Research,* May, Vol. IX, pp. 209-213.

87. Kenneth J. Roering and Carl E. Block, (1976), "Population Density and type of Purchase of Explanatory Variable in Consumer Information Search." *Journal of the Academy of Marketing Science* Vol. 4 (4), (Fall), pp. 731-741.

88. Terrence O'Brien, (1977), "Informational Handling in Consumer Decisions." of the *Academy of Marketing Science,* Vol. 5 (3), (Summer), pp. 229-232.

89. Chester R. Wasson, (1979), "Consumer Choice Process : Search or Autometic Responses". *Journal of the Academy of Marketing Science,* Vol.7 (4), (Fall), pp. 360-373.

90. Robert A.Westbrook, (1979), "Patterns of Information source Usage Among Durable Goods Buyers". *Journal of Marketing Research,* Vol XVI. (August). pp. 303-312.

91. Dennis M. Crites, John A. Shaw and Sak Onkvist, (1979), "Information Source Usage By Prospective Home Buying Consumers" *Journal of the Academy of Marketing Science.* Vol. 7 (2), pp. 80-94.

92. Brain T. Ratchford, (1980), "The Value of Information for Selected Applances", *Journal of Markeitng Research,* February, Vol. XVII (1), pp.14-25.

93. Hans B. Thorelli and Jack L. Engledow, (1980), "Information System : A Policy Prospective", *Journalof Marketing,* Vol. 44 (2), (Spring), pp. 9-27.

94. Geoffrey C.Keil and Roger A.Layton, (1981), "Dimensions of Consumer Information Seeking Behaviour". *Journal of Marketing Research,* May ,Vol. XVIII (2), pp. 233-239.

95. Calvin P. Duncan and Olshavsky, (1982), "External Search : The Role of Consumer Beliefs." *Journal of Marketing Research,* February, Vol. XIX, pp. 32-43.

96. Naresh K. Malhotra, Arun K. Jain, and Stephen W. Lagakos (1982). "The Inforamtion Overload Controversy: An Alternative Viewpoint." *Journal of Marketing*, Vol. 46 (2), (spring), pp. 27-37.

97. Chin Tiong Tan, and Iraj Dolich, (1983), "A Comparative Study of Consumer Information Seeking: Singapore VS U.S." *Journal of the Academy of Marketing Science,* Vol. 11(3), pp. 313-322.

98. J.G.Udell, (1966), "Pre-purchase Behaviour of Buyers of Small Electrical Applications", *Journal of Marketing,* October,Vol. 30, pp. 50-52.

99. James F.Engel, David T.Kollat and Roger D.Blackwell, (1978), Consumer Behaviour. Third ed., The Dryden press, Hinsdale, Ill: ionis, p. 392.

100. George Katona, (1960), The powerful consumer, McGraw Hill, Inc., New York, p.123.

101. Leon G. Schiffman and Leslie Lazar Kanuk, (1990), "Consumer Behaviour", New Delhi: Prentice-Hall of India Private Limited, (3rd ed.,), p.67.

102. William H. Peters, (1970), "Relative Occupational Class Income: A Significant Variable in the Marketing of Automobiles". *Journal of Marketing,* April, Vol. 34 (2), pp. 74-77.

103. Myers J.H., R.R. Stanton and A.F. Hung, (1971), "Correlates of Buying Behaviour: Social Class VS. Income." *Journal of Marketing,* October, Vol.35 (4), pp. 8-16.

104. Terrence V. S'Brien. "Tracking Consumer Decision Making", *Journal of Marketing,* Vol. 35 (1), pp.34-40.

105. Robert B. Settle, (1972), "Attribution Theory and Acceptance of Information". *Journal of Marketing Research,* February, Vol. IX (1), pp. 85-88.

106. Zarre V. Lambert, (1972), "Price and Choice Behaviour." *Journal of Marketing Research,* February, Vol. IX (1), pp. 35-40.

107. Leo Bogart and Charles Lehman, (1973), "What Makes a Brand Name Familiar." *Journal of Marketing Research,* Vol. X, pp. 17-22.

108. Joseph W. Newman, and Richard Werbel, (1974), "Automobile Brand Loyalty." *Journal of the Academy of Marketing Science,* Vol. 2 (4), (Fall), pp. 593-601.

109. Lesig V. Parker and Thomas P. Copley, (1974), "Consumer Beliefs, Attitudes and Brand Preferences". *Journal of the Academy of Marketing Science.* Vol. 2 (2), (spring). pp. 357-366.

110. David R. Wheller, (1974), "Brand Loyalties : Qualitative Quantitative or Both." *Journal of the Academy of Marketing Science,* Vol. 2(2), (Fall), pp. 651-657.

111. George Tesar Gerald G.Udell and G.M. Naidu, (1974), "The Role of Marketing in the Introduction of Technologically New Products : The Case of the Electric Car". *Journal of the Academy of Marketing Science.* Vol. 2 (4), (Fall), pp. 642-650.

112. Lessig V. Parker and Beverlee B. Anderson, (1974), "Do Different Consumers Operate Under the Same Preference Model". *Journal of the Academy of Marketing Science,* Vol 4(1), (winter), pp. 429-439.

113. Donald J. Hempel, (1975), "Family Role Structure and Housing Decisions". *Advances in Consumer Research,* Vol. 2, pp. 71-80.

114. Ach G. Woodside, (1975), "Effects of Prior Decision–making, Demographics, and Psychographics on Martial Roles for purchasing Durables". *Advances in Consumer Research,* Vol. 2. pp. 81-92.

115. Marilyn M. Dunsing A. Jeane L. Haftstrom, (1975), "Methodological Consideration in Family Decision Making Studies." *Advances in Consumer Research,* Vol. 2, p. 172.

116. Walter A. Henry, (1976), "Cultural Values Do Correlate Withy Consumer Behaviour." *Jouranl of Marketing Resaearh,* May Vol. XIII (2), pp. 121-127.

117. Richard D. Nordstrom and John E. Swan, (1976), "Does a Change in Customer Loyalty Occur When a New Car Agency is Sold." *Journal of Marketing Research,* May, Vol. XIII (2), pp.173-177.

118. Peter J. Paul and Michael J. Ryan, (1976), "An Investigaton of Perceived Risk at the Brand Level". *Journal of Marketing Reseach,* May ,Vol. XIII (2), pp. 184-188.

119. Clint B. Tankersly, (1977), "Attitude and Brand Loyalty : A Longitudinal Study of Multi-attribute Attitude Models and

Interverrening Vaiables". *Journal of the Academy of Marketing Science,* Vol. 5(3), (summer), pp. 249-262.

120. Rom J. Markin, (1979), "The Role of Rationalisation in Consumer Decision Making Process: A Revisionist Approach". *Journal of the Academy of Marketing's Science*. Vol. 7 (4), (Fall) pp. 316.

121. Linda L. Golden, (1979), "Consumer Reaction to Explicit Brand Comparisons in Advertisement". *Journal of Marketing Research,* November, Vol. XVI, pp. 517-532.

122. Naresh K. Malhotra, (1981), "A Scale to Measure Self-Concepts Person Concepts, and Product Concept". *Journal of Marketing Research,* November, Vol.XVIII (4), pp. 456-464.

123. William J. Qualls, (1981), Changing Sex Roles "Its Impact Upon Family Decision Making". *Advanced in Consumer Research,* Vol. IX, pp. 267-270.

124. Richard J. Rexeisen, (1981), Is there a Valid Price Quality Relationship, *Advances in Consumer Research,* Vol. IX, p. 190.

125. Jon B. Freuden and Douglas S. Bible, (1982), "The Home Purchase Process: Measurement of Evaluative Criteria Through Pair wise Measures". *Journal of the Academy of Marketing Science.* Vol. 10 (4), (Fall), pp. 359-376.

126. Gilles Laurent and Jean-Noel Kapferer, (1985), "Measuring Consumer Involvement Profiles". *Journal of Marketing Research,* February, Vol. XXII (1), pp. 41-53.

127. Albert J. Della Bitta, Kent B. Monrose and John Marketing. Mc Ginnis, (1981), "Consumer Perceptions of Comparative Price Advertisement", *Journal of Marketing Research,* November, Vol. XVIII (4), pp. 45.

128. Srinivasan. T.C, (1987), An Integrated Approach to Consumer Research, Vol. XIV, pp. 96-100.

129. Ronald P. Hill, (1987), "The Buying Process: Effects of and on Consumer Mood States". *Advances in Consumer Research,* Vol. XIV, and p. 435.

130. Ravichandran M., (1988), "Consumer Perceptions and Purchase Decisions". A Study of Urban and Semi Urban Consumers of Durable Goods. Unpublished ph. D Dissertation, Department of Comerce, University of Madras (June).

131. O.P. Gupta and P.N. Abrol, (1995), "Dictionary of Commerce", Anmol Publications, New Delhi, (2nd ed.), p. 86.

132. R.S.N. Pillai and Bagavathi, (1987), "Marketing", S. Chand & Co., New Delhi, (1st ed.), p. 348.

133. O.P. Gupta, Op.Cit., p.104.

134. O.P. Gupta, Op.Cit. p.143.

135. David L. Loudon, Op.Cit, p.17.

3

Description of the Study Area

For proper understanding of the consumer behaviour and their decision, a brief analysis of the study area is become inevitable. It would give the necessary background for the analysis; besides, it would provide an answer to the question like why the consumers behave in certain ways. The description of the study area deals with a brief history of Vellore district, location, physical features like topography, soil, flora and fauna, climate and rain fall, demographic features like population, sex ratio, age wise classification, SC and ST population, density of population, occupation, literacy, urbanization, classes of towns, agricultural development, land use pattern, size of the holdings, crop pattern, irrigation, sources of irrigation, industrial development, large scale industries, small scale industries, cottage industries, place of leather industry in Vellore district, infrastructure development like roads, railways, electricity consumption, housing, financial institutions, commercial banks, co-operative banks, source of finance, standard of living of the people – Television per thousand persons, telephone connections, computers, internet connections, two wheelers, four wheelers used, health indications – doctors, beds, hospitals.

BRIEF HISTORY OF VELLORE DISTRICT

The present, newly formed, "Vellore District", is carved out from the erstwhile North Arcot Ambedkar district of

Tamil Nadu. Vellore district was also known as "Thondaimandalam region" in early South Indian History. The pages of South Indian History are replete with incidences that the region has witnessed many thrilling fights for supremacy between the local chieftains and rulers on the one hand and the French and English. On the other hand, the places of historical importance in this district are Arcot, Vellore and Wallajapet.

LOCATION

The geographical area of Vellore District is 6077 sq.km. And it lies between $12^0\,15^1$ and $13^0\,15^1$ of northern latitude and $78^o\,20^1$ and $79^0\,50^1$ of the Eastern longitude. It is bounded on north by Chittor district of Andhra Pradesh, on the south by Tiruvannamali district and on the west by Dharmapuri district and on the East by Thiruvallur and Kancheepuram district. The western parts of the District are endowed with pleasing hilly sceneries like Yelagiri Hills, but rocky bases mostly cover the eastern side of the District. The location of the Vellore could be seen in the Map kept at fig.3.1 below.

PHYSICAL FEATURES

The Javadi Hills represent the loftiest mountain range in this district. The general height of the Javadi hills is 2,500 feet with peaks rising up to 4,200 feet. The Yelagiri hills lie in the north – western part of Tirupattur Taluk. There are many hills of lower elevation, which lie scattered in Vellore, Vaniyambadi, Gudiyattam, Arcot and Walajapet taluks.

TOPOGRAPHY

The district is covered mostly by rocky hills. The spherical rock masses of these hills throw off rainwater without retaining them, helping to generate a number of hill streams feeding a number of tanks.

SOIL

The soil in the district is mostly of the red ferruginous variety, both sandy and loamy, with black area accounting

Fig. 3.1 : Map of Vellore District

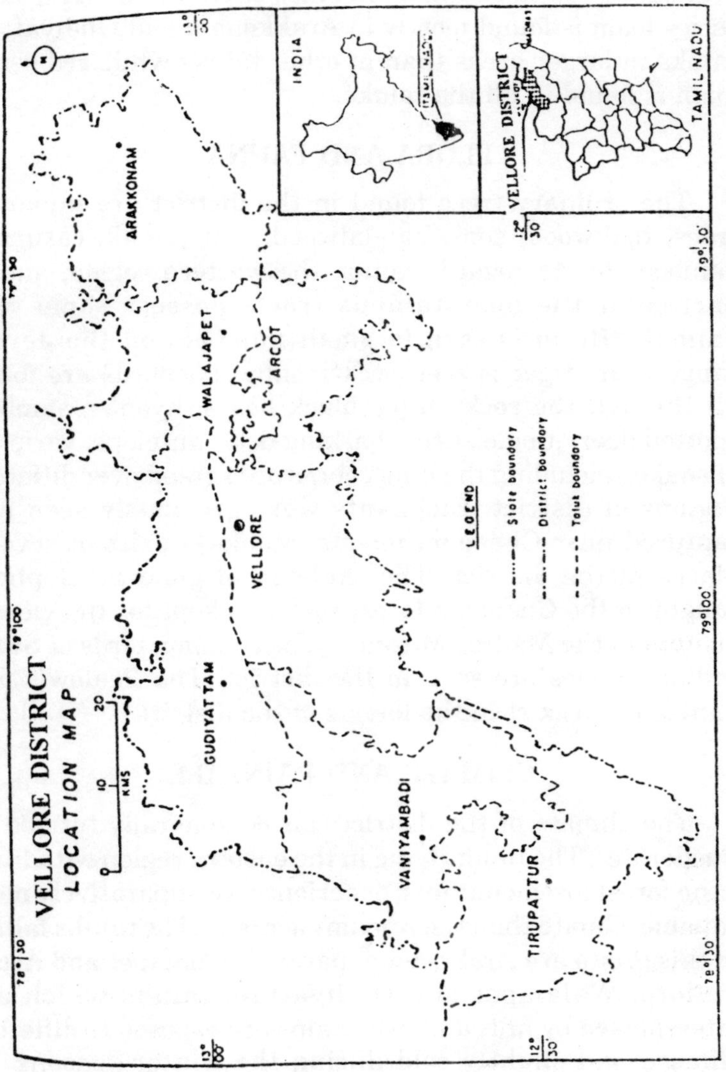

for about 16 per cent .The black soil is found mostly in the neighborhood of the rivers of Palar, Ponnai and in the ayacuts of a few big tanks. The black series clay occurs in Gudiyattam, Walajapet, Arcot, Arakkonam and Vellore taluks. The black series loam is found mostly in Arakkonam and Gudiyattam taluks in larger areas than in other taluks while red series loam is found in all the taluks.

FLORA AND FAUNA

The ordinary trees found in the district are tamarind trees, teakwood, some sandalwood, ven – teak, casurina, bamboo etc. As regards fauna, the western region, and in particular the mountainous tracts possess some wild animals. Bison is seen in small numbers on the Javadi ranges, and tiger is seen occasionally. Leopards are found all through the rocky hills, black bears, hyenas, sambar, spotted deer, jungle sheep, barking deer, antelope, varieties of snakes including the king cobras are spread over different regions of district. Elephants were previously seen and captured near Chengam forests. Monkeys exist in several places in the district. The skeleton of gigantic elephant caught in the Chengam forest region is kept for the view of visitors in the Madras Museum. The common birds of South Indian species are seen in the district. The Peafowls and Jungle fowls exist in the forests of the district.

CLIMATE AND RAINFALL

The climate of the district can be generally termed as "moderate". The taluks lying in the eastern region with litter or no forest are mountains; experience a comparatively more equable climate than the remaining areas. The taluks falling in this group are Arakkonam, parts of Walajapet and Arcot, Vellore, Walajapet and Gudiyattam taluks which are interspersed by hills and mountains are exposed to different climate and slightly cold during the winter seasons. In Tirupattur and Vaniyambadi taluks, climate is rather slightly cold during winter, but moderate during the other seasons.

Table 3.1 : The Rainfall Distribution in Vellore District between 1995 and 2000

(mm)

S.No.	*Month*	*Normal*	*1995*	*1996*	*1997*	*1998*	*1999*	*2000*
1.	January	30.9	28.05	-	-	-	8.9	-
2.	February	8.9	4.05	-	-	-	1.1	47.9
3.	March	11.5	11.82	1.60	-	-	-	-
4.	April	24.3	0.45	53.60	14.00	18.50	20.5	24.4
5.	May	70.8	250.15	9.60	52.50	20.80	53.9	51.8
6.	June	58.1	93.52	144.90	130.50	23.20	56.8	60.5
7.	July	87.6	131.20	34.20	56.20	104.80	30.8	70.3
8.	August	132.9	270.90	156.60	103.40	181.30	85.5	130.7
9.	September	160.5	111.10	161.10	102.90	211.30	73.9	219.7
10.	October	166.2	99.60	150.90	117.60	159.00	142.3	210.7
11.	November	158.4	36.80	131.40	183.50	212.30	105.2	68.0
12.	December	61.0	13.80	277.60	84.40	100.20	56.9	60.0
	TOTAL	971.1	1051.44	1121.50	934.90	1031.40	635.8	964.0
	Deviation-%	-	+8	+15	-4	+6	-34	-7

(**Source :** Dept. of Agriculture, Vellore.)

The climate of the district is basically tropical. The average minimum and maximum temperature in the district are 16 degrees Celsius and 38 degrees Celsius respectively. The rainfall is received mainly during the North East and Southwest monsoons. During the year 2000, the district received a rainfall of 964 mm against a normal rainfall of 971.1 mm.

The above table reveals that the heaviest rainfall 1121.50 mm (+15) was recorded during the year 1996 while the lowest 635.8 mm (-34) was recorded during the year 1999.

RIVERS

The following rivers, Palar, Pennar, Pennai, Pambar, Malattar, Kavundinyanadi, and Goddar are the major sources of drainages in Vellore District. These rivers are mostly dry and sand waste. Palar, rising near Nandidurg in Karnataka, enters the district in the western part through Vaniyambadi Taluk. It flows then in an east – north – easterly direction in the Taluk and is joined by some jungle streams like Malattar flowing in Gudiyattam Taluk. The river forms the boundary between Vaniyambadi, Gudiyattam and Vellore taluks. After cutting across Walajapet taluk, it runs along the boundary between Walajapet and Arcot taluks as also Arakkonam and Cheyyar taluks before entering Chengalpattu district on the east. Ponnai river, which is a tributary of Palar river, rises in Chittor district of Andhra Pradesh. It flows on the western part of Walajapet taluk and joins Palar near Ranipettai. The rivers, Goddar and Kavundinyanadi, which flow from north to south in Gudiyattam.

DEMOGRAPHIC FEATURES:

Population

The total population of the district as per 1991 Census was 30,26,432. Vellore is the ninth most populous district in Tamilnadu. The details of population as per Census 1991 are furnished in table 3.2 below.

Table 3.2 : Demographic Features of Vellore District

S. No.	*Particulars*	*Male*	*Female*	*Total*	*%*
1.	Rural	10,48,055 (50.71)	10,18,663 (49.29)	20, 66,718 (100.00)	68
2.	Urban	4,81,889 (50.21)	4,77,825 (49.79)	9,59,714 (100.00)	32
	Total population	15,29,944 (50.55)	14,96,488 (49.45)	30,26,432 (100.00)	100
3.	SC Population	3,15,119 (50.24)	3,12,199 (49.76)	6,27,398 (100.00)	21
4.	ST Population	25,384 (50.91)	24,473 (49.09)	49,857 (100.00)	2
	Literate population				
5.	Rural	6,13,581 (62.95)	3,61,205 (37.05)	9,74,786 (100.00)	32
6.	Urban	3,37,362 (56.46)	2,60,144 (43.54)	5,97,506 (100.00)	20
	Total literate	9,50,943 (60.48)	6,21,349 (39.52)	15,72,292 (100.00)	52

(**Source :** District Statistical office, Census 1991, Vellore.)

Out of the total population, 68 per cent of the people are living in rural areas and 32 per cent are living in urban areas. Though the percentage of urban population is above the national average, it is below the state average. The Scheduled Caste population in Vellore district accounted for 21 per cent according to 1991 census and the Scheduled Tribe population accounted for 2 per cent. According to 1991 census, 32 per cent of the rural population and 20 per cent of the urban population are literate. The density of population in Vellore district is calculated as 498 and the average size of household in the district is 4.90. The percentage of workers to total population is 37.93 per cent. The percentage of female workers to total population is only 10.58.

Growth of Population in Vellore District

The growth of population in Vellore district between 1991 and 2001 is calculated and presented in table 3.3 below.

Table 3.3 : Growth of Population in Vellore District Between 1991 and 2001

Sl.No.	*Particulars*	*1991*				*2001*			
		Male	*Female*	*Total*	*%*	*Male*	*Female*	*Total*	*%*
1.	Rural	1048055	1018663	2066718	68	1085192	1079462	2164654	62
2.	Urban	481889	477825	959714	32	658679	659637	1318318	38
	Total	1529944	1496488	3026432	100	1743871	1739099	3482970	100
	Literate								
3.	Rural	613581	361205	974786	32	750250	545855	1296105	37
4.	Urban	337362	260144	597506	20	516731	433216	949947	27
	Total	950943	621349	1572292	52	1266981	979071	2246052	64
	Growth rate	(36.69)	(38.05)	(37.37)		(88.58)	(73.68)	(81.1)	

(**Source :** District Statistical office, Census 1991 and 2001,Vellore.)

Table 3.3 reveals that the total population in Vellore district has increased from 3026432 in 1991 to 3482970 in the year 2001, an increase of 15.08 per cent, which is higher than the state growth rate during the same period. During this period, the percentage of rural population has declined to 62 per cent; the percentage of urban populations has increased to 38 percent. The literacy rate for both rural and urban areas has increased. The sex ratio in Vellore district, according to 2001 Census, is 997/1000 males, which is higher than the state average sex ratio.

Occupational Pattern

The occupational pattern of the people of the Vellore District as per 1991 Census is given below.

As can be seen in Table 3.4, 30.96 per cent of the working population belonged to agriculture labourers, and the cultivators constitute 21.97 per cent. Thus, agriculture is the main source of livelihood of the people in the district. Non-workers, who depend upon the workers for their living, account for 59.58 per cent of the total population, showing a dependency (dependents on workers) ratio of more than unity.

Urbanization in Vellore District

According to 1991 Census Report, 32 per cent of the people in Vellore District have been living in urban centers. The process of urbanization has been taking place very fast in this district. The table 3.5 presents the towns, their status and populations.

There are nine municipal towns and 15 town panchayats in Vellore District.

Classification of Towns

The towns in Vellore District have been grouped and graded according to the size of populations as per 1991 Census and presented in table 3.6 below.

The nine towns with municipal administration and their location in the district could be seen in the map kept at fig. 3.2. below.

Table 3.4 : Occupational Pattern of People in Vellore District

Sl. No.	*Items*	*Males*	*Females*	*Total*	*Percentage*
1.	Cultivators	210640	58094	268734	21.97
2.	Agricultural Labourers	199411	179359	378770	30.96
3.	Workers : Livestock, Forestry, etc.,	5403	1339	6742	0.55
4.	Workers: Mining & Quarrying	1749	520	2269	0.19
5.	Workers: Maf. & Pro. In H.H.Ind.	55297	24774	80071	6.55
6.	Workers: Maf. & Pro. Other than H.H.I.	107341	17879	125220	10.24
7.	Construction Workers	253 62	2040	27402	2.24
8.	Trade & Commerce Workers	87420	5821	93241	7.62
9.	Transport, Storage & Common Workers	36889	654	37543	3.07
10.	Workers in other services	98214	29836	128050	10.46
11.	Marginal Workers	5124	70077	75201	6.15
12.	Total Workers	1223243	832850	390363	100
13.	Non- Workers	697094	1106095	1803189	59.58
	Total	1529944	1496488	3026432	100

(**Source :** District Statistical Office, Census 1991,Vellore)

Note : Percentage in row 1 to 11 is to the total number of workers in row 12 and percentage of non-workers is to total population.

Administrative Divisions.

Vellore district is divided into three development divisions viz; Vellore development division, Tirupattur development division and Ranipet development division for administrative purposes.

Table 3.5 : Name of the Towns, Status and Population in Vellore District

Sl. No.	*Name of the Town / Status of Administration*	*Population*
1	2	3
	A. Municipalities	
1.	Ambur	75,911
2.	Arakkonam	71,928
3.	Arcot	45,205
4.	Gudiyattam	83,232
5.	Ranippettai	42,583
6.	Tirupattur	55,282
7.	Vaniyambadi	72,428
8.	Vellore	175,061
9.	Walajapet	26,972
	B. Town Panchayat	
10.	Allapuram	21,424
11.	Darapadevedu	21,207
12.	Gandhi Nagar (Katpadi Extension)	9,364
13.	Jolarpettai	23,719
14.	Kalinjur	11,369
15.	Kaveripakkam	12,756
16.	Melvisharam	26,613
17.	Pallikondai	18,672
18.	Panapakkam	8,826
19.	Peranambattu	36,195

Contd....

Table 3.5 : (Contd....)

Sl. No.	*Name of the Town / Status of Administration*	*Population*
1	2	3
20.	Sattuvacheri	25,165
21.	Shembakkam	9,739
22.	Sholinghur	21,412
23.	Torappadi	9,480
24.	Udayendram	10,421
	ALL TOWNS	914964

(**Source :** District Census Hand Book, 1991, Tamil Nadu.)

Table 3.6 : Classes of Towns in Vellore Districts

Sl.No.	*Population*	*Class*	*No. of Towns*
1.	100,000 and above	I	1
2.	50,000 to 99,999	II	5
3.	20,000 to 49,999	III	10
4.	10,000 to 19,999	IV	4
5.	5,000 to 9,999	V	4
6.	Below 5000	VI	–
	Total		24

(**Source :** District Census Hand Book, 1991, Tamil Nadu.)

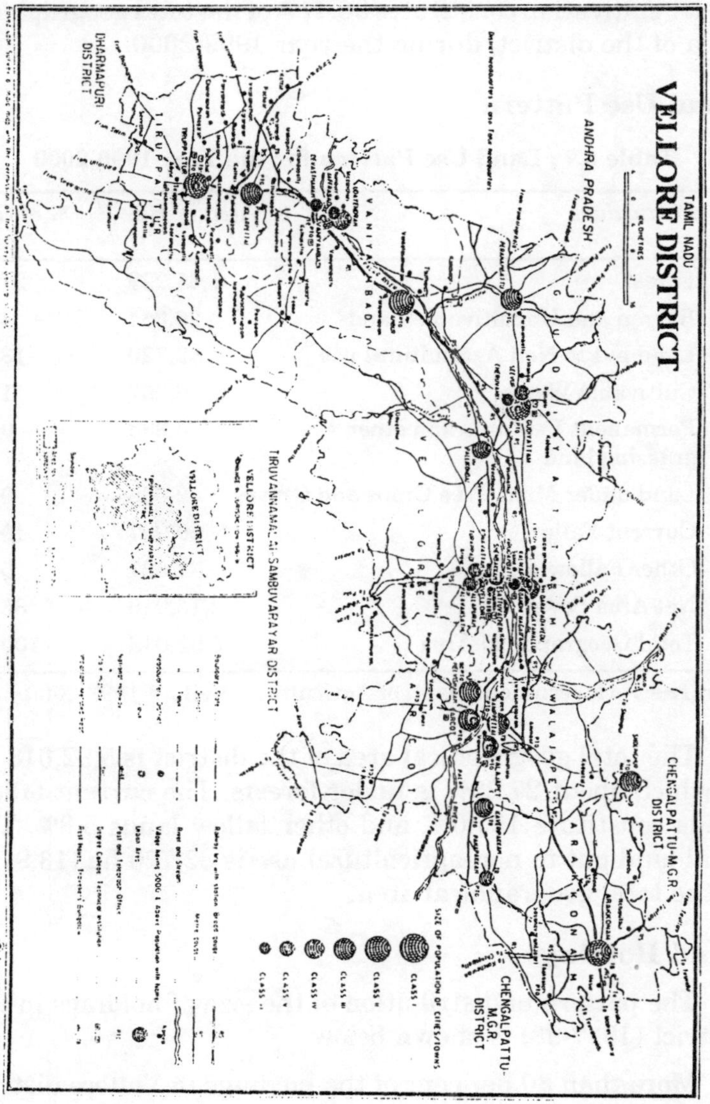

Fig. 3.2 : Map of Towns in Vellore District

AGRICULTURAL DEVELOPMENT.

The district is predominantly agricultural. The net area under cultivation constitutes 36.47% of the total geographical. area of the district, during the year 1999-2000.

Land Use Pattern

Table 3.7 : Land Use Pattern for the Year 1999-2000

Sl. No.	*Particulars*	*Area in Ha.*	*% of Geo. area*
1.	Forest	1,61,229	27.23
2.	Barren and Uncultivable Lands	26,054	4.40
3.	Land put to Non Agricultural use	82,720	13.97
4.	Cultivable Waste	6,757	1.14
5.	Permanent Pastures and other grassing land	3,833	0.65
6.	Land under Misc. Tree Crops and Groves	2,685	0.45
7.	Current Fallow	60,997	10.30
8.	Other Fallow	31,827	5.38
9.	Net Area Sown	2,15,916	36.47
10.	Total Geographical Area	5,92,018	100.00

(**Source :** Government Dept. of Agriculture, Vellore 1999-2000.)

The total geographical area of the district is 5,92,018 ha of which about 27.23% is under forests. The current fallow lands constitute 10.30%, and other fallow lands 5.8%. The total land put to non-agricultural use is 82,720 ha (13.97%) of the total geographical area.

Land Holdings

The pattern of distribution of the size of holdings in the district (1997-98) is shown below.

More than 80 per cent of the holdings in Vellore district are less than one hectare. But these large numbers of smallholdings possess only 41.78 per cent of the total area. As the size of holdings expand, the number of holdings are decreasing.

Table 3.8 : Size Distribution of Land Holdings

Sl. No	Size of Land Holdings	Numbers	%	Area in Ha.	%
1.	Less than 1 ha	339260	80.06	119896.93	41.78
2.	1-2 ha	58242	13.74	79225.43	27.61
3.	2-5 ha	23305	5.50	657135.42	22.90
4.	More than 5 ha	2964	0.70	22135.42	7.71
	Total	423771	100	286971.33	100

(**Source :** District Statistical Hand Book, Vellore, 1997-98.)

Irrigation

The sources of irrigation in the district are wells, canals and tanks. The area irrigated through various sources of irrigation during 2000-2001 is presented in table 3.9 below:

Table 3.9 : Sources and Area of Irrigation

Sl. No.	Source of Irrigation	No.	Irrigation Capacity (ha)		Irrigated area (ha)	
			Gross	Net	Gross	Net
1.	Govt.Canals (1067km)	604	8337	9512	865	985
2.	Tanks	1355	45287	57581	20272	23812
3.	Wells	119699	117944	92275	117944	92275
	Grand Total		216855	216949	159353	140884

(**Source :** Govt. Return 1999-2000, Dept. of Statistics,Vellore.)

There are 92,275 wells, 23812 tanks, and 985 Govt. canals in Vellore district, and they are the major sources of irrigation.

Cropping Pattern

The cropping pattern as has shown below gives the crops grown in the farm at a particular point of time. The area under production of crops during the year 2000-2001 is furnished in Table 3.10 below.

Table – 3.10 : Cropping Pattern

(Area in ha)

Sl. No.	*Crops*	*2000-2001* *Area in ha*	*Production in Tons*
	A. Food Crops		
1.	Paddy	52,332	2,35,562
2.	Millets	37,184	52,253
3.	Pulses	37,242	23,906
	Sub Total	1,26,758(58%)	3,11,721
	B. Non-Food Crops		
4.	Cotton	4,962	1,754
5.	Sugar Cane	27,249	2,45,241
6.	Oil Seeds	59,592	1,01,575
	Sub Total	91.803(42%)	3,48,570
	Grand Total	2,18,561(100%)	6,60,291

(**Source :** Dept.of Agriculture, Vellore 2000-2001.)

Note : The figures in the parentheses are the percentages to the total in each column.

The area under food crops command 58 percent of the total cropped area compared to 42 per cent of the non-food crops. The important food crops grown in the district are paddy, millets and pulses. Cotton, sugar cane and oil seeds are the important non-food crops grown by the farmers in Vellore district. The production of various crops in the district indicates that paddy tops among other food crops. Among the non-food crops, sugarcane stands first followed by oilseeds.

INDUSTRIAL DEVELOPMENT

The District offers ample scope for the development of agro-based industries. The District has the required raw materials, backward and forward linkages, and training center.

Large Scale Industries

The District is fast developing into an important industrial region of the State. There are 919 *Large and Medium Scale* factories in this district, concentrating on the following items of industrial activity.

* Fertilizer Production
* Chemicals
* Textile products
* Sugar/Jaggery manufacturing
* Asbestos manufacturing
* Explosives manufacturing
* Finished Leather & Leather
* Footwear for export.
* Manufacture of food products
* Steel casting
* Synthetic fibers
* Auto bearing manufacturing
* Color TV manufacturing
* Tyres & Tubes manufacturing
* Food processing
* Cement production

Small Scale Industries

The Vellore District has a large number of small-scale industries. The small-scale industries are grouped under 18 categories, as presented in table 3.11 below.

Table – 3.11 : Small Scale Industries in Vellore District

Sl. No.	*Details of Classification of Industry group*	*Numbers*
1.	Food Products	1,711
2.	Beverages, Tobacco and Tobacco Products	149
3.	Cotton Textiles	333
4.	Wool, Silk and Synthetic Fibre Textiles	122
5.	Jute, Hemp and Mesta Products	7
6.	Hosiery and Ready-made Garments	2598
7.	Wood and Wooden Products	498
8.	Paper and Paper Products	519
9.	Leather and Fur Products	1,021
10.	Rubber and Plastic Products	344
11.	Chemicals and Chemical Products	1,110
12.	Non-Metallic Mineral Products	344
13.	Basic Metals & Alloy Industries	229
14.	Metal Products and Parts	1,013
15.	Machinery and Parts except Electrical Machinery	967
16.	Electrical Machinery and Apparatus	956
17.	Transport Equipment and Parts	506
18.	Other Manufacturing Industries	1,216
	Total	13,643

(**Source :** Dept. of Economics and Statistics, Chennai-6.)

The hosiery and ready-made garments have the largest number of units. Food products, manufacturing, chemical products, leather and leather products, machinery etc follow it.

Khadi & Village Industries

The Khadi & Village Industries Board plays a very important role in promoting industrial development in Vellore district. The Khadi & Village Industries units are presented in table 3.12 below:

Table 3.12 : Khadi & Village Industries Units in Vellore District

Sl.No.	*Category*	*Number of Units*
1.	Khadi Units	25
2.	Village Industries	10
3.	Co-operative Societies	12
4.	Villages Spinning Units	15

The kadhi units, largest in the category, have 25 units. The other categories of industries, which have large number of units, are: village spinning units, co-operative societies, and village industries.

Employment

The employment in public and private sector is furnished in table 3.13 below:

Table 3.13 : Public Sector and Private Sector Employment in Vellore Districts

(In Numbers)

Category	*1993-94*	*1994-95*	*1995-96*	*1996-97*	*1997-98*
Public Sector	118176 (74.57)	119267 (72.88)	125204 (72.08)	130085 (71.08)	124793 (70.56)
Private Sector	40303 (25.43)	44376 (27.12)	48487 (27.92)	52933 (28.92)	52080 (29.44)
Total	158479	163643	173619	183018	176873

(**Source :** Director of Employment and Training, Chennai – 5.)

The public sector employees more labourers compared to the private sector. But due to the change in Government policy, the importance of public sector has gone down. As a result, the employment in the public sector is declining. But the activation of private sector generates more employment.

Leather Industries in Vellore District

Leather industry plays a very vital role in Vellore district. It provides employment opportunities to the people, and revenue for the development of the district.

TRADE AND COMMERCE

Vellore district is an important commercial center. Most of the in and out movement of trade is carried through road transport by lorries and carts drawn by bullocks. The mercantile consignments include all items from iron and steel and sundry shopping goods. Most of the commodities that move out of the district are general goods, grains, sugar, jaggery, fertilizers and chemicals.

The Commercial Banks, Co-operative Banks and Private Leading Moneylenders provide finance for the trade. The outlets for consumer goods consist of Co-operative consumer stores.

INFRASTRUCTURE DEVELOPMENT

Roads

Roads connect all the villages in the district. The details of road length in kilometers during 2000 – 2001 are given in above Table 3.14 below:

Table 3.14 : Length of Roads

Sl.No.	*Details*	*Length (km)*
1.	Mud Road	33.14
2.	Metal Road	171.19
3.	Tar Road	2571.45
4.	Cement Concrete Road	99.60
5.	Corporation & Municipal Roads	452.22
6.	Panchayat Union & Panchayat Roads	3176.32
7.	Town Panchayat & Township Roads	421.58
8.	Village Roads	131.25
9.	State Highways	531.00
10.	National Highways	191.00
	Total	7778.75

(**Source :** District Statistical office, Vellore.)

Motor Vehicles

The motor vehicles on road, classified as Commercial and Non-Commercial Vehicles, are presented in table 3.15 below.

There are 14,262(10.69%) Commercial Vehicles as against 1,19, 175(89.31%) Non-Commercial Vehicles on road in Vellore district by the end of the year March -2001.

Railways

In vellore district of Tamil Nadu, the railway lines run all through, from north to south and from west to east. The railway route between Chennai and Jolarpet is a busy one, and also an important one, from the point view of the economy, as well as connectivity with the rest of the nation.

Though Jolarpet is a small town, but it gains its importance because of its railway junction. All the trains that ply to north India, west India, northeast India and south India pass through Jolarpet Junction. From Jolarpet, one can reach any part of India by train. Besides passenger trains, a number of cargo trains too pass through Jolarpet. At this junction, goods wagon, destined to different parts of India, are separated and are linked with other goods trains. This facility of separating the wagons is a unique one and is not available at other junctions.

Other important junctions in the district are Katpadi and Arakkonnam. At Katpadi, trains leaving for Andra Pradesh are diverted. At Arakkonnam, trains, destined for west India like Bombay, pass through.

The district of Vellore has to its credit 197 km of broad gauge line and 56 km of meter gauge line. The main train routes leading to Kerela and Bangalore are electrified. This has made the people of Vellore district move faster and quicker.

Electricity and Power

The Mettur Hydro–Electric Power and the Madras Thermal Power Stations meet the energy needs of this

Table 3.15 : Registered Motor Vehicles in Vellore District (As on 31st March 2001)

Sl.No.	*Items*	*Number*
	A. Commercial Vehicles	
1.	Stage Carriers-Public	914
	Private	400
2.	Mini Bus	2
3.	Auto Rickshaw	3216
4.	Ordinary Taxi	76
5.	Motor cab-State	236
	All India	107
6.	Maxi cab-state	436
	All India	11
7.	Omni Buses-state	6
	All India	5
8.	Private Service vehicle	120
9.	Light commercial vehicle	289
10.	Lorry-state permit	5423
	National permit	1635
11.	School Buses	31
12.	Ambulance	39
13.	Fire Fighter	20
14.	Articulated vehicle-state	121
	National	26
15.	Tractor and Trailor	1149
	Sub Total	14262
	A. Non-Commercial Vehicles	
16.	Motor cycle	26218
17.	Scooter	14054
18.	Mopeds	65306
19.	Tri-cycle	96
20.	Motor car	9711
21.	Jeep	1097
22.	Station wagon	5
23.	Tractor	2454
24.	Three wheeler	48
25.	Four wheeler	90
26.	Road Rollers	11
27.	Others	85
	Sub Total	119175
	Grand Total	133437

(**Source :** Commissioner of Transport, Chennai-5.)

district. The distribution of power is made through the electricity systems of Chengalpattu, Vellore and Thiruvanamalai towns. There is a very good network of power transmission lines in the district. As on 2000-01, all the census towns, villages, hamlets and Adi – Dravidar colonies of the district were given power connection. Barring very few places, which are either interior or inaccessible areas, where there is little or no demand for power, the district enjoys power connection in all areas.

The details of consumption of electricity in Vellore district during 2000-01 in each category are presented below:

Table 3.16 : Category Wise Power Consumption in Vellore district

Sl.No.	Category	(In Million Units)	Percentage
1.	Domestic	4472	15.48
2.	Commercial	2676	9.27
3.	Public Lighting	400	1.39
4.	Industrial	12482	43.22
5.	Agricultural	7680	26.60
6.	Miscellaneous	1166	4.04
	Total	28876	100.00

(**Source :** District Statistical office, Vellore.)

It can be seen from the above that consumption of power is the highest in respect of industries with 43.22% in Vellore district and agriculture with 26.6% is the next important category, and the lowest in respect of public lighting with 1.39% during the year 2000-01.

Housing

The following table gives the details about the housing development in Vellore district.

Table 3.17 : Housing Developing in Vellore District

Slum	EWS	Lig	Hig/Mig	TNGRH	Police	Anc	SIHS	Total
-	4591	6273	8059	1622	-	-	-	20545
	(22.35)	(30.53)	(39.23)	(7.89)				(100)

SLUM : Slum Clearance / Improvement Housing Scheme.
EWS : Economically Weaker Section.
LIG : Low Income Group Housing Scheme.
MIG/HIG : Middle Income Group, High Income Group.
TNGRH : Tamil Nadu Govt. Servant Rental Housing Scheme.
Police : Police Housing Scheme.
ANC : Ancillary Service Scheme.
SIHS : Subsidized Industrial Housing Scheme.
Source : Tamil Nadu Housing Board, Chennai-35.

Out of the 20,545 houses, constructed up to 31st March, 1998, 39.23 per cent of the houses belonged to MIG / HIG category, followed by LIG 30.53 per cent, EWS formed 22.35 per cent, and TNGRH accounted for 7.89 per cent.

Financial Institutions

The District is served by 199 Commercial Bank branches, besides branches of District Central Co-operative Bank Limited., Tamil Nadu State Agriculture and Rural Development Bank, Urban Co-operative Banks, and Tamil Nadu Industrial Investment Corporation.

The Vellore Central Co-operative Bank is the most important financial agency extending credit facilities to the agriculturists through its 343 Primary Co-operative Societies. In many cases, short-term loans are converted into medium and long-term loans for various reasons including drought, to help the farmers repay the loans with least inconvenience.

Urban Co-operative Banks of the district are under the control of the Joint Registrar of Co-operative Societies,

Vellore. It has 13 branches in taluk headquarters and extends jewel loan facilities to the agriculturists.

The Vellore district branch of the Tamil Nadu Co-operative State Land Development Bank meets the long-term credit requirements of the agriculturists through 17 Primary Land Development Banks in the district. The overdue position in these banks is very high. The poor recovery hampered the operations of these institutions to a very large extent. However, due to revised regulation of advances, the bank is able to meet not only the term-loan requirements of agriculturists but also the allied activities of the small and marginal farmers in large number.

Regional Distribution of Commercial Banks.

The regional distribution of commercial banks is furnished in Table 3.18.

Table-3.18 : Regional Distribution of Commercial Banks in Vellore District.

		Distribution of Commercial banks Distribution of Branches as on March, 2001				
Sl.No.	*Type*	*No.of Banks*	*Rural*	*Semi-urban*	*Urban*	*Total*
1.	State Bank and Associates	4	20	12	6	38
2.	Public Sector Banks	14	68	42	17	127
3.	Private Sector Banks	11	15	8	11	34
	TOTAL	29	103	62	34	199

(**Source :** District Statistical office, Vellore.)

In Vellore district the regional distribution of commercial banks shows that they are in favour of rural areas. Thanks to the nationalization of banks.

Distribution of Bank wise Consumption Loan

There is a great demand for consumption loan in Vellore district. It is mainly for the purchase of durable products and to meet the expenditures in connection with ceremonies. The table below gives the bank-wise distribution of consumption loans in Vellore district during the year 2001-02.

Table 3.19 : Bank Wise Distribution of Consumption Loans During 2001-02

Sl.No.	*Name of the Bank*	*Consumption Loans (Amount Rs. in 000's)*			
		A/C	*UNIT*	*Amount*	*%*
1.	Canara Bank	2	2	350	2.06
2.	Dhananlakshmi Bank	4	4	4	0.02
3.	Indian Bank	34	34	.130	0.76
4.	Indian Overseas Bank	23	23	360	2.13
5.	State Bank of India	320	320	3020	17.76
6.	VCC Bank	1	1	300	1.76
7.	Urban Co-operative Bank	4980	4980	12836	75.51
	Total	5364	5364	17000	100

(**Source :** Indian Bank –District Credit Plan, 2001-02.)

Out of the total loan of Rs.1,70,00,000, the Urban Co-operative Banks have sanctioned 75.51 per cent of the consumption loans as against 17.76 per cent by the State Bank of India. It reveals that most of the people living in urban areas are the borrowers of consumption loans mainly for the purchase of home durable products.

Small Savings Collections

The small saving is an important component of development. The small saving drives have been undertaken every year. The net amount collected from such drives is furnished below.

Table 3.20 : Small Saving Collection (Net) in Vellore District form 1992-93 to 1997-98.

(Rs. In Crores)

1992-93	*1993-94*	*1994-95*	*1995-96*	*1996-97*	*1997-98*
15.27	22.15	27.48	18.29	14.65	19.89

(**Source :** Director of Small Savings, Chennai-6.)

The small saving collection in Vellore district has not been steady between 1992-93 and 1997-98. Though the collection has increased from Rs.15.27 crores in 1992-93 to Rs.27.48 crores in 1994-95, it declined to Rs18.29 crores in 1995-96 and it further declined to Rs14.65 crores in the year 1996-97. But it picked up during the year 1997-98.

HEALTH INDICATORS

Hospitals like educational institutions are service organizations. Efficient and successful management of these institutions are essential for the creation of a healthy society. There are 13 Government Hospitals in Vellore District with 1637 beds and 179 doctors. The population per bed accounted for 2128 and the population per doctor accounted for 19,458. During the year 2001-02, there were 64 Primary Health Centers, functioning all over the district. Besides Government Hospitals, there are private hospitals, mostly located in urban centers. The Christian Medical College and Hospital, located at Vellore, is a multi specialty hospital not only in India but also in Asia.

STANDARD OF LIVING OF THE PEOPLE

The standard of living of the people could be judged by items of food they consume, the types of clothes they clad, and other durable goods they consume. The average telephone connections in Vellore was recorded as 5.05 per cent, of the population, telephone users accounted for 56 / 1000, television 583 / 1000, computers 7 / 1000, and internet users 4 /1000. Though 50 per cent of the population views television, in the consumption of other items of information technology, the district remains at a very low level, but there is a sign of improvement in their consumption.

4
Methods of Study

INTRODUCTION

The methods used for analyzing the consumer behaviour are presented in this chapter. It deals with the choice of the study area, selection of sample consumers, selection of durable products, sampling procedure, collection of data, data requirements, and tools of analysis.

CHOICE OF THE STUDY AREA

Vellore district, one of the largest districts in Tamil Nadu State, has been purposively selected for the present study. The features of the Vellore district have been presented in the previous chapter.

URBAN CENTERS

There are nine Municipal towns, scattered all over the Vellore district. The study is confined to urban consumers, therefore, all the Municipal towns were listed in descending order. Out of the nine Municipal towns, top four Municipal towns with largest number of dealers were selected. Accordingly, the four Municipal towns selected for the study includes: Vellore Municipal town – district Headquarters, Gudiyatham, Vaniyambadi, and Tirupattur are the Taluk Headquarters of the respective taluks.

SELECTION OF DURABLE PRODUCTS

As shown in the previous chapter, the levels of living of the people in the towns and urban centers have been fast changing. The consumerist attitude has been fast catching up in this area. It is evident from the number of durable products possessed by the consumers. Though the middle and upper middle income group of households possessed a number of durable products, only four durable products have been chosen for the present study because of two reasons: (i) the consumers of these products tend to collect more information about these products, and (ii) the consumers of these products exercise choice before taking the purchase decision. The durable products chosen for the present study are : Television, Refrigerator, Air-cooler, and Washing machine.

CHOICE OF CONSUMERS

The selection of consumers of durable assets was routed through the dealers of the above durable products.

IDENTIFICATION OF DEALERS

The dealers in the above four durable products belonging to the four Municipal towns were identified in the first stage. There were 10 dealers belonging to Vellore Municipal towns, with more than one lakh population, 10 dealers from Tirupattur town and 5 dealers form the other two towns, with five dealers each. Altogether, there are 30 dealers of the durable products in the sample.

IDENTIFICATION OF CONSUMERS

From the selected dealers of durable products, 20 consumers who purchased the durable goods from them were identified. While the consumers purchased the said item from the given dealers, the researcher, who spent nearly six months to distribute the questionnaire to the consumers, served the questionnaire to them. Thus the ultimate sample frame comprises of 600 (30 X 20=600) consumers of selected durable products. The consumers were asked to return the filled-up questionnaires to the dealers from whom they bought the durable products. Only 450 filled-up questionnaires were received back. The distribution of shops and the number of consumers consulted and the return of the filled-up questionnaires are presented in table 4.1 below. The distribution of shops and the sample consumers of durable products in selected towns is also shown in fig. 4.1.

Table 4.1 : Distribution of Shops and the Sample Consumers of Durable Products in Selected Towns

Sl. No.	*Name of the Town*	*No. of Dealers*	*Total Number of Consumers to Whom Questionnaires Served*	*Question-naires Received Back*	*Percen-tage*
1.	Vellore	10	200	150	33.33
2.	Gudiyatham	5	100	75	18.89
3.	Vaniyambadi	5	100	85	16.67
4.	Tirupattur	10	200	140	31.11
	Total	30	600	450	100.00

Note : Durable products: Television, Refrigerator, Air-cooler, and Washing machine.

Fig. 4.1 : Distribution of Shops and the Sample Consumers of Durable Products in Selected Towns

Percentage

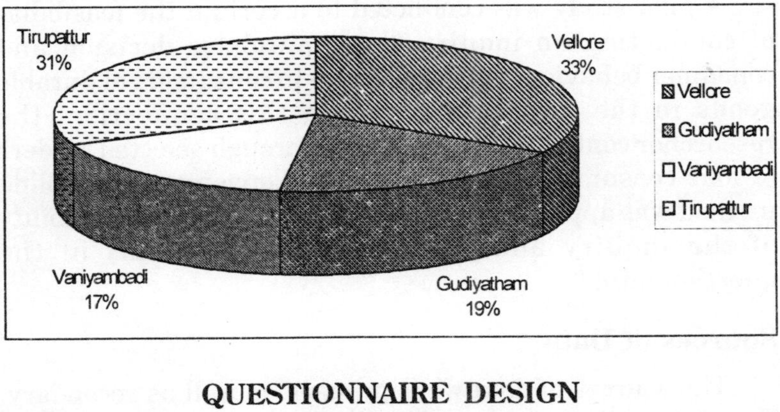

QUESTIONNAIRE DESIGN

The purchases of the durable products belonged to middle and upper middle class, and as they were educated, hence, it was decided to use questionnaire to collect the required details from them. Accordingly, the questionnaire with covering letter was handed over personally to the consumers through selected dealers and they were requested to return the filled in questionnaire after a period of 20 days. The respondents took 20 to 45 days to return the completed questionnaires.

Structured Questionnaire

A structured questionnaire was prepared for the study, with two sections. Section-A of the questionnaire was framed to obtain general information about the information sources used by the consumers, the particular sources of information in the search process, the evaluation criteria used in making the final decision, and the factors influencing the consumers in the decision-making process. The section-B was to incorporate general information about the consumers of four durable products. The draft questionnaire was tested with 50 consumers and the exercise ensured the adequacy of the questions in the questionnaire. Moreover, adequate care was taken to see that the consumers had not misunderstood the questions, and were sufficiently informed to give the answers.

Pilot Study

A pilot study was conducted to ascertain the feasibility of conducting an inquiry about purchase decision and consumer behaviour, with reference to consumers of durable goods in the Vellore district. In this connection, the researcher contacted 30 consumers through selected traders of four consumer durable products. Convenience sampling method was applied. The study had confirmed the feasibility of the inquiry and the quality of the items in the questionnaire.

Sources of Data

The sources of data were primary as well as secondary. The data collected from the consumers survey constitute primary and the information gathered from books, journals, magazines, reports, dailies were secondary. The data collected from both these sources were scrutinized, edited, and tabulated.

PERIOD OF STUDY

The inquiry was conducted with the consumers of durable items from January to July 2002.

TOOLS OF ANALYSIS

The data collected from respondents were edited, classified, and analysed with the following tools. The study had used simple averages and percentages. Simple statistical tests like Chi-Square test was applied to bring out the association of variables. Principal Component Analysis and Factor Analysis were used to identify the factors involved in purchase decision. The Analysis of Discrimination was used to find out the differences among variables with respect to the consumers decision and their perception.

ANALYSIS OF PERSONAL DATA

The personal data collected from the consumers of the selected durable consumer products were classified and presented below.

Age of Respondents

The respondents were classified according to their age as presented in table 4.2 below.

Table 4.2 : Age-wise Classification of Respondents

Sl. No.	*Age (years)*	*No. of Respondents*	*Percentage*
1.	< 30	20	4.44
2.	31-40	95	21.11
3.	41-50	180	40.00
4.	> 50	155	34.45
	Total	450	100.00

As shown in the above table, there are 20 respondents, below 30 years of age, 95 respondents belonged to 31 to 40 years, 180 respondents belonged to 41 to 50 years, and 155 respondents are above 50 years of age. The age group of consumers of durable products chosen for the study is also shown in Fig, 4.2.

Fig. 4.2 : Age-wise Classification of Sample Consumers

Percentage

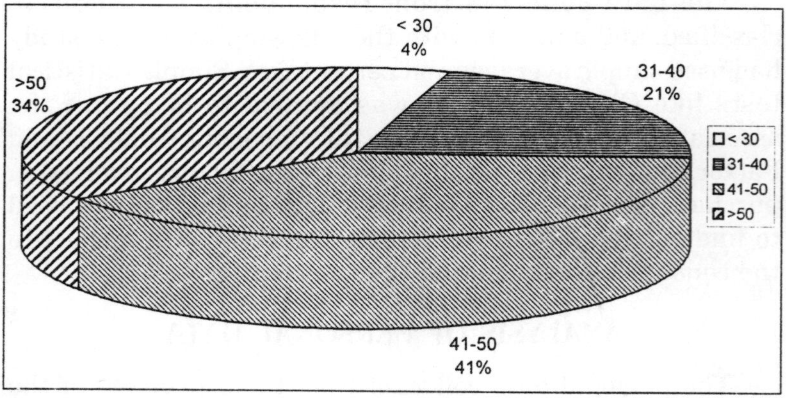

Classification of Respondents According to Gender

The gender plays a vital role in the selection of consume durables in any household. The classification of respondents according to gender is presented in table 4.3 below.

Table 4.3 : Gender-wise Classification of Respondents

Sl. No.	*Gender*	*No. of Respondent*	*Percentage*
1.	Male	174	38.67
2.	Female	276	61.33
	Total	450	100.00

The gender-wise classification shows that female consumers dominate among the respondents with 61.33 percent over the male consumers. The gender- wise classification of respondents chosen for the study is also shown in Fig, 4.3.

Fig. 4.3 : Gender-wise Classification of Sample Consumers

Percentage

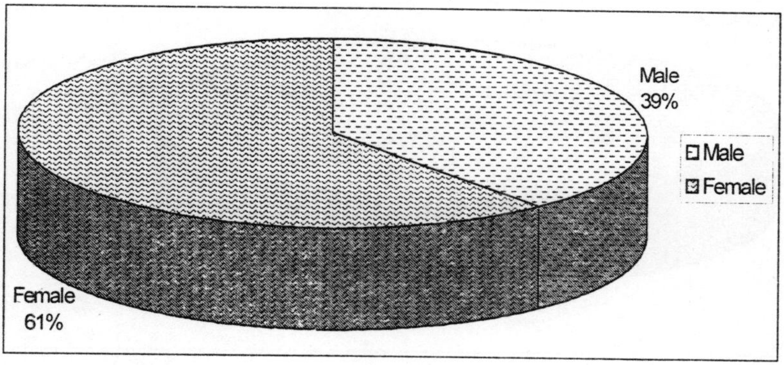

Educational Pattern of the Respondents

The level of education of the sample consumers of durable products is presented in table 4.4 below.

Table 4.4 : Level of Education of the Sample Consumers

Sl. No.	*Level of Education*	*No. of Respondents*	*Percentage*
1.	SSLC	175	38.88
2.	HSC	123	27.33
3.	Graduate	124	27.56
4.	Professional	28	6.22
	Total	450	100.00

As shown in the above table, those who studied S.S.L.C formed the majority of the sample consumers with 175 (38.88 per cent). They are followed by graduates 124 (27.56 per cent), and those who studied H.S.C. 123 (27.33 per cent). The professionals form 28(6.22 percent) of the total sample consumers. There are no illiterate in the sample consumers.

The level of education of the sample consumers chosen for the study is also shown in Fig. 4.4.

Fig. 4.4 : Level of Education of the Sample Consumers

Percentage

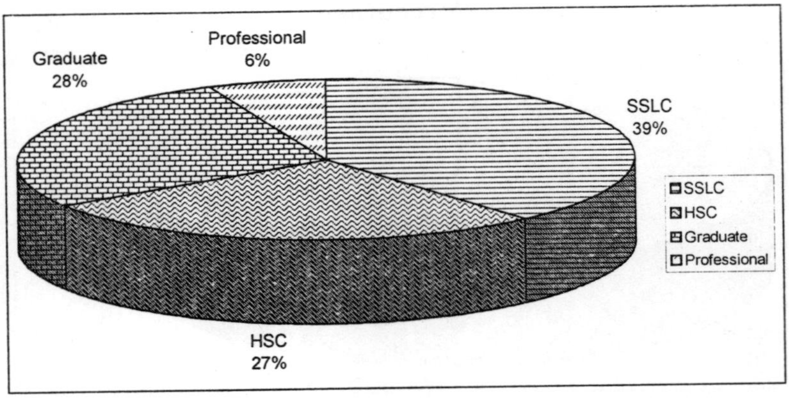

Occupational Pattern of the Respondents

The level of education decides the occupation of a person. Generally, more qualified persons hold higher posts. Table 4.5 presents the occupational classification of selected respondents.

Table 4.5 : Occupation-wise Classification of the Respondents

Sl. No.	*Occupation*	*No. of Respondents*	*Percentage*
1.	Public sector	56	12.44
2.	Private sector	274	60.89
3.	Professional	43	9.56
4.	Farming	37	8.22
5.	Business	40	8.88
	Total	450	100.00

Those who are working in public sector include Government Departments also. They are 56 (12.44 per cent). There are 274 (60.89 per cent) respondents who worked in private sector particularly in tanneries. The professionals include doctors, engineers, lawyers, charted accountants 43 (9.56 percent). The farmers and businessmen included in the sample are self-employed people who form 37 (8.22 percent) and 40 (8.88 percent) respectively. The occupational pattern of the respondents chosen for the study is also shown in Fig, 4.5.

Fig. 4.5 : Occupational Pattern of Sample Consumers Percentage

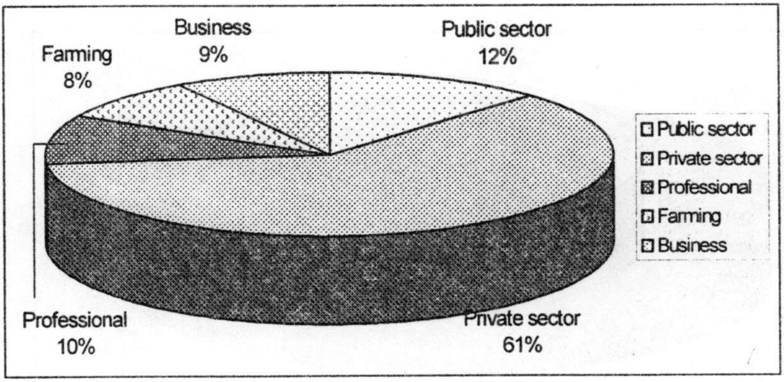

Income Pattern of the Respondents

Table 4.6 presents the classification of the respondents according to income.

Table 4.6 : Income-wise Classification of Respondents

Sl. No.	*Monthly Income (Rs)*	*No. of Respondents*	*Percentage*
1.	< 5000	40	8.89
2.	5001-8000	220	48.89
3.	8001-11,000	143	31.78
4.	> 11,000	47	10.44
	Total	450	100.00

As shown in the above table, the highest group i.e., 220 (48.89), consumers belonged to the income bracket of 5001 to 8000. It is followed by 143 consumers (31.78per cent) whose monthly income falls in the category of Rs.8001 to 11,000. 40 consumers' (8.89per cent) monthly income is below Rs5000. There are 47 consumers (10.44per cent) in the sample whose monthly income is above Rs11, 000. The income pattern of the sample consumers chosen for the study is also shown in Fig, 4.6.

Fig. 4.6 : Income Pattern of Sample Consumers

Percentage

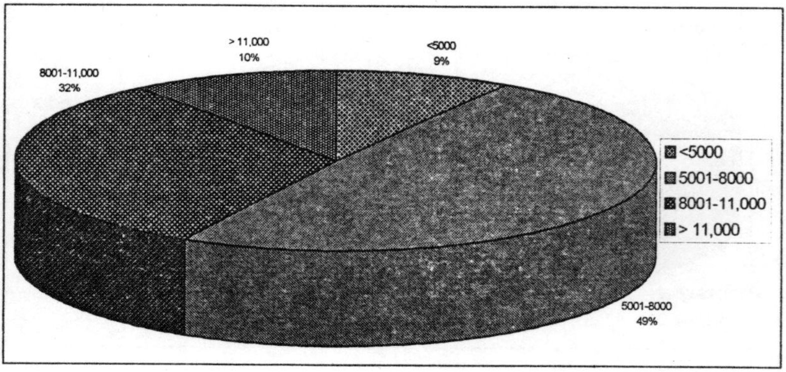

With the above basic details of the consumers, the data relating to the information sources and the consumer's choice are analysed and the results are discussed in the following chapters.

5
Results and Discussion

The problems regarding the purchase decision and consumer behaviour were analysed, and the objectives were presented in the first chapter. The important concepts used in the study were reviewed and presented in the second chapter. The profile of the study area, Vellore District, was presented in the third chapter. The methods of study were presented in the fourth chapter. The present chapter V, deals with the results of the primary data collected on the consumer behaviour, and it is discussed with the specific objectives. This chapter is divided into two sections. First section deals with information sources, and pre-purchase behaviour of the consumers, and evaluative criteria in purchase decisions is dealt in the second section.

The factors influencing the consumer's decision making process form part of the sixth chapter.

The details of sources of information and the pre-purchase decision were collected from 450 sample consumers. The information, furnished by the sample consumers, are classified and analysed below.

The previous chapter two provided a conceptual view in understanding of different consumer information sources and their importance. The information sources are grouped into three broad categories for the purpose of this study, viz., (i) personal sources, (ii) commercial sources and (iii) retail outlet sources.

The following are the groups of information sources under three headings:

Personal Sources	*Commercial Sources*	*Retail Outlet Sources*
Past Experience	Advertisement in News Papers, Pamphlets etc.,.	Sales men
Friends, Relatives, Neighbours etc,.	Magazines, books	Personal shop visits and retail outlet
Personal observation and examination	Consumer Reports Radio, Television Road side hoardings/ posters etc.,. Movie (Cinema)	

INFORMATION SOURCES AND PRE-PURCHASE BEHAVIOUR

It has been set as the first objective of this study to examine the relative importance of the information sources used by the consumers in the purchase of four consumer durable products. In addition, the relationship between information sources and certain selected variables are examined. The variables selected are (i) the time lag between contemplation and actual purchase, (ii) the level of planning in that time gap, (iii) the number of shops, dealers and showrooms visited, (iv) the number of brands considered at the time of making the choice by the consumer and (v) certain personal characteristics like age, sex, education, income, and occupation of the consumer. The above-mentioned variables, in one way or the other, are relevant to all consumers, irrespective of the sources of information. So, both the users and non-users of the above sources of information are relevant for this purpose.

Thus the focus in this chapter will be to find out the relationship between these variables and the information sources.

Relative Importance of the Source of Information

While bringing out the relative importance of the three sources of information, weightage is given to answers of all the four products selected for the study. Hence chi-square test was used to determine the association between variables.

The total population sample consists of 450 consumers and each answer is for four products, totaling 1800 answers. Analysis is done based on the total number of answers in order to make maximum use of consumers' views.

One way of expressing the importance of source is in terms of exposure and subsequent attention. This is probably the most commonly used criterion[1].

One must be very cautious, however, in judging one medium to be more important than another simply because a greater percentage of people report attending it. This does not necessarily indicate that the source under consideration proved to be helpful in making a purchase decision. As a consequence, there can be significant difference between exposure and effectiveness (i.e., actual use of the information)[2].

So a consumer may gather information from one source, and that source need be or need not be helpful to him in the final stage of his taking the decision. A consumer might have received first information from one source. But it is quite possible that this source may or may not be that important when he actually takes the decision to buy. In this study, the focus will be on exposure and effectiveness, in order to bring out the relative importance of the different sources.

The consumers were asked to indicate the source from which they got the information (exposure) in the first instance regarding the product, its features viz, price, design, colour, availability etc. Then they were asked about the source, which they actually used at the time of taking the purchase decision (effectiveness.)

Exposure to Information Sources

It could be seen in Table 5.1 that nearly 68.44 percent of the total responses point out that the commercial source of information gave the first information to know the products. So, from the exposure point of view, commercial source is the important source in total population. Next comes the retail outlet source, which accounts for 23.5 percent of the consumer responses. Personal source is considered to be the least important source, and it covers only 8.06 percent, and so it can be concluded that in the earlier stages of decision process the commercial source is the most important source in providing the information to consumers. The frequency distribution of information sources used based on exposure for the study is also shown in Fig. 5.1.

Table 5.1 : Frequency Distribution of Information Sources Used (Based on Exposure)

Sources	*Refrigerator*	*Television*	*Air cooler*	*Washing Machine*	*Total*	*Percentage to total*
Personal	35	50	40	20	145	8.06
Commercial	320	316	298	298	1232	68.44
Retail outlet	95	84	112	132	423	23.50
Total	450	450	450	450	1800	100.00

(**Source :** Primary Data).

Effectiveness of the Information Sources

While measuring the effectiveness of the three sources of information for consumers, which could be seen from Table 5.2 that the commercial source is used more than the other sources by the consumers in making the final choice. The commercial source accounted for 55.44 percent, and next comes the retail outlet source, which covered 32.95 percent. The personal source 11.61 percent is the least important source for the sample population in helping to make the purchase decision. The frequency distribution of information sources used based on effectiveness is also shown in Fig. 5.2.

Fig. 5.1 : Exposure to Information Sources

Percentage

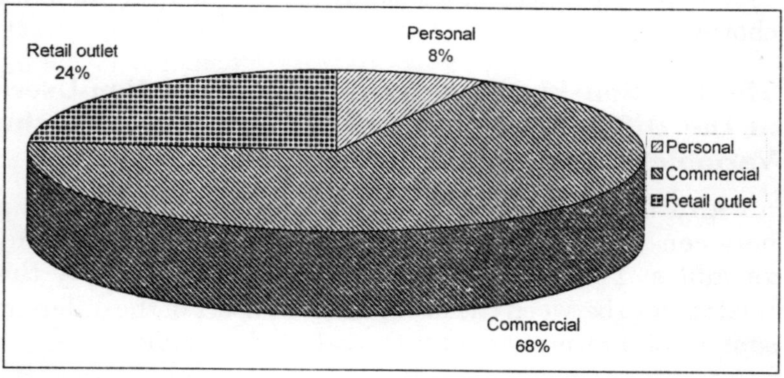

Table 5.2 : Frequency Distribution of Information Sources Used (Based on Effectiveness)

Sources	*Refrige-rator*	*Tele-vision*	*Air cooler*	*Washing Machine*	*Total*	*Percentage to total*
Personal	35	42	60	72	209	11.61
Commercial	297	248	255	198	998	55.44
Retail outlet	118	160	135	180	593	32.95
Total	450	450	450	450	1800	100.00

(**Source :** Primary Data)

Fig. 5.2 : Exposure to Information Sources

Percentage

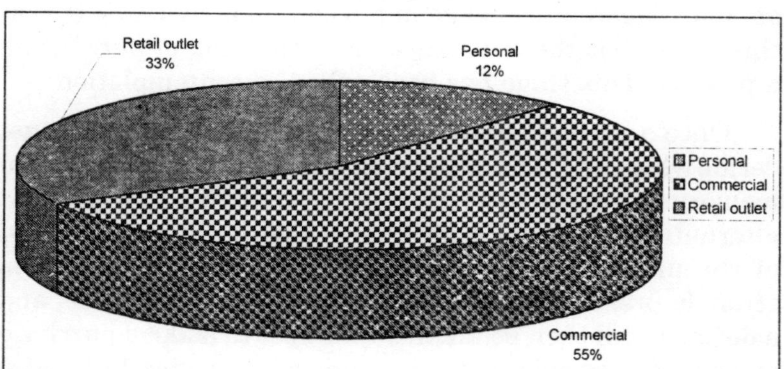

It could be concluded from the above analysis that commercial source of information is the most important source for consumers in the study area in making the final choice.

The Relationship Between the Users and Non-Users of the Different Sources of Information with the Variables Selected

An attempt may now be made to find out the relationship between the information sources and some important variables. The purpose of such analysis is to study the relationship between the users and non-users of the different sources of information with the selected variables.

Time Lag Between Contemplation and Actual Purchase

The time taken by the consumer from the time he first thought of purchasing a product to actual purchase is the next important question. In other words, it can be said that it is time lag between problem recognition process and actual purchase process. The first step in any type of consumer decision process is problem recognition. This occurs when an individual perceives a difference between an ideal and actual state of affairs at any given point of time. When it occurs, the human system is energized, and goal orientation begins. Seemingly unrelated activities now become organized to satisfy this state of arousal. In short, the system is turned on and triggered to engage in purposeful activity. So it is at this stage that the consumer starts thinking of purchasing a product. This stage has been called as contemplation.

Once a problem is recognized, then the consumer must decide what to do. The initial step is an internal search within memory to determine whether or not enough is known about alternatives to permit some kind of choice. Often, one brand of the product, what he thought of purchasing, will be strongly preferred to others, based on past experience, and a decision will then be taken on the spot to make a purchase as early as possible. If the consumer is not able to finalize his choice within the internal search, then it is more probable that he will look into external search making use of variety of information sources available to him.

The information sources chosen will vary from individual to individual, and from one situation on another. Search refers to the process whereby a consumer seeks (collects) information to learn about the advantages and disadvantages of the various alternatives, to satisfy a problem that has become recognized[3]. Whether search will occur or not, and the extent to which it occurs, depend on the consumer's perceptions of the benefits and the costs involved. Costs included are time, money, psychological discomfort, and the dangers of information overload.

An analysis to find out whether there is significant difference in time taken between the users and non-users of particular information is attempted now.

The frequency distribution of time taken and the information sources used and not used by total consumers are given in Table 5.3.

Table 5.3 : Frequency Distribution of Time Taken and Information Sources Users and Non-Users (In Percentage)

Number of Weeks Taken	*Personal Sources*		*Commercial Sources*		*Retail Outlet Sources*	
	Users	*Non-Users*	*Users*	*Non-Users*	*Users*	*Non-Users*
One week	22.16	18.32	27.50	15.72	18.21	26.00
Four weeks	36.31	26.50	11.02	38.97	32.79	12.21
Eight weeks	15.72	18.27	12.23	21.85	08.92	19.76
More than eight weeks	25.81	36.91	49.25	23.46	40.08	42.03
Total	100.00	100.00	100.00	100.00	100.00	100.00

(**Source :** Primary Data.)

From Table 5.3, it could be said that there is no significant difference between the users and non-users of personal source of information, while the difference is more between the users and non-users of commercial and retail outlet source of information in total population. For instance, the difference is more than 27 percent when the time taken is one to four weeks in relation to commercial source, and about 21 percent in the case of one to four weeks in relation to retail outlet source.

It could also be noticed from the same Table that among the users, majority (58 percent) of the personal source users took one to four weeks, while the users of the commercial source took more than four weeks (61 percent) and retail outlet (51 percent) source took one to four weeks (based on cumulative percentage).

The significant difference between the users and non-users with time taken can also be verified by applying the chi-square test and the results are given in Table 5.4, 5 and 6.

Table 5.4 : Information Sources and Time Taken (Independent Test for Personal Sources)

Personal Sources	*Time Taken*			*More than Eight Weeks*
	One-Week	*Four-Weeks*	*Eight-Weeks*	
Users	62	93	68	91
Non-Users	336	389	256	529
Total	398	482	324	620

Chi-Square Test

Degree of freedom	*Chi-square value*	*Table value @ 1% level*
4	8.235	13.28

(**Source :** Primary Data).

Applying the chi-square test at 1 per cent level, the table value of x^2 for d.f. 4 are 13.28. The calculated value of x^2 is 8.235 for personal source, which is less than the table value.

Table 5.5 : Information Sources and Time Taken (Independent Test for Commercial Sources)

Personal Sources	*Time Taken*			*More than*
	One-Week	*Four-Weeks*	*Eight-Weeks*	*Eight Weeks*
Users	206	312	217	272
Non-Users	192	170	107	348
Total	398	482	324	620

Chi-Square Test

Degree of freedom	*Chi-square value*	*Table value @ 1% level*
4	69.91	13.28

(**Source :** Primary Data).

Table 5.6: Information Sources and Time Taken (Independent Test for Retail Outlet Sources)

Personal Sources	*Time Taken*			*More than*
	One-Week	*Four-Weeks*	*Eight-Weeks*	*Eight Weeks*
Users	92	46	42	184
Non-Users	306	436	282	436
Total	398	482	324	620

Chi-Square Test

Degree of freedom	*Chi-square value*	*Table value @ 1% level*
4	81.85	13.28

(**Source :** Primary Data).

It can be said that there is no significant difference in time taken between the users and non-users of personal source of information in total population. In other words, it could be said that time taken is independent in relation to personal source of information. While examining the relationship of commercial source with time taken, the computed value of x^2 is 69.91, which is higher than the table value, proving that there is significant difference in time taken between the users and non-users of commercial source of information. The same result is also indicated for the retail outlet source in which the calculated value of x^2 is 81.85, which is greater than the table value. It can be said that time taken is dependent on both commercial and retail outlet source of information.

From the above analysis, it could be concluded that in the sample time taken is less when personal source is used, and more when the other two sources are used. In bringing out the relationships time taken is independent in the samples with relate to personal sources. It is dependent in total population, which relate to commercial source, and retail outlet source of information.

Level of Planning in that Time Gap

It has been explained that time lag between contemplation and actual purchase may differ among consumers, due to several reasons. Planning plays a major role in taking any decisions. A consumer, before making his purchase, has to think and plan different aspects, relating to that purchase. Planning for a purchase decision means the different activities the consumer does, regarding collection of information from various sources, the financial outlay, the varied users of the product that he can make for himself or for his family and so on. How much a consumer planned to select a brand, and how much it is influenced by different information sources is considered next. So an attempt is made here to find out whether there is significant difference in level of planning between the users and non-users of different sources of information.

The levels of planning and information sources used and not used by consumers are likewise examined and the frequency distribution is presented in Table 5.7. From the Table, it could be noticed that there is a difference between

Table 5.7 : Frequency Distribution of Level of Planning and Information Sources Users and Non-Users (In percentage)

Level of Planning	*Personal Sources*		*Commercial Sources*		*Retail Outlet Sources*	
	Users	*Non-Users*	*Users*	*Non-Users*	*Users*	*Non-Users*
(i) Planned very Carefully	56.76	40.78	48.71	46.38	56.01	47.13
(ii) No planning but took few days	27.00	22.52	21.32	24.57	21.00	26.00
(iii) No planning at all	13.14	22.72	19.76	8.31	9.45	12.19
(iv) No planning but waited for finance	3.10	13.98	10.21	20.74	13.54	14.68
Total	100.00	100.00	100:00	100.00	100.00	100.00

(**Sources:** Primary Data).

the users and non-users of all the information sources in relation to level of planning; particularly the variation is very high (about 16 percent) in personal source when the consumers planned very carefully. It can also be noticed that among the users, all the users of personal (84 percent), commercial (70 percent) and retail outlet (77 percent) sources planned carefully for their purchase activities. The relationship is also tested by chi-square test, the results of which are presented in Table 5.8, 9, and 10.

It could be seen from Table that at 1 percent level for d.f. 5 the table value of X^2 is 15.09. The calculated value of X^2 for personal source of information is 102.45 which is greater than the table value and for commercial and retail outlet sources and also their calculated values are 51.6 and 603.2 which are greater than the table value. So it could be said that level of planning is dependent on the three information sources.

Table 5.8 : Information Sources and Level of Planning (Independent Test for Personal Sources)

Personal Sources	*Level of Planning*			*No Planning but Waited for finance*
	Planned very Carefully	*No Planning but took Few Days*	*No Planning at all*	
Users	612	503	85	47
Non-Users	78	31	43	23
Total	690	534	128	70

Chi-Square Test

Degree of freedom	*Chi-square value*	*Table value @ 1% level*
5	102.45	15.09

(**Source :** Primary Data).

Table 5.9 : Information Sources and Level of Planning (Independent Test for Commercial Sources)

Commercial Sources	*Level of Planning*			*No Planning but Waited for finance*
	Planned very Carefully	*No Planning but took Few Days*	*No Planning at all*	
Users	287	178	84	18
Non-Users	403	356	44	52
Total	690	534	128	70

Chi-Square Test

Degree of freedom	*Chi-square value*	*Table value @ 1% level*
5	51.6	15.09

(**Source :** Primary Data).

From the above analysis, it could be concluded that all the users of the three information sources in the populations planned carefully for their purchases. In bringing out the relationships, the information sources and the level of planning are dependent on each other.

Table 5.10 : Information Sources and Level of Planning (Independent Test for Retail outlet Sources)

Retail Outlet Sources	*Level of Planning*			*No Planning but Waited for finance*
	Planned very Carefully	*No Planning but took Few Days*	*No Planning at all*	
Users	512	52	24	00
Non-Users	178	482	104	70
Total	690	534	128	70

Chi-Square Test

Degree of freedom	*Chi-square value*	*Table value @ 1% level*
5	603.2	15.09

Number of Shops, Dealers, Showrooms Visited

In the external search, the consumer involves in collecting more information about products. He visits a number of shops, dealers, and showrooms to know more about the market nature. As already mentioned, if he has finalized his brand after problem recognition, he may not spend his time in visiting many shops. But even if he has finalized the brand, he has to choose the shop from which he is going to purchase. For this purpose, he may visit a number of shops. He also makes decisions about stores, shops, and other retail outlet about the type of stores, special showrooms, discount shops etc. The consumer determines the shop where he has to make the purchase and it will be based on several important factors like location, price, discount, service etc. So in order to collect this information, he visits more number of shops, dealers and showrooms to finalise his store choice.

This function of visiting different shops for taking a purchase decision differs among consumers. An attempt is made here to find the significant difference, if any, between the users and non-users of the three information sources, with reference to number of shops, stores, dealers visited by the sample consumers.

The frequency distribution of the number of shops, showrooms visited in relation to information sources are presented in Table 5.11. It can be inferred from the above table that among the users, about 55 percent of personal source users, 54 percent of commercial sources users and 47 percent of retail outlet source users visited one or two shops at the time of making the purchase. While the users of retail outlet source visited more than two shops, which accounted for the same 44 percent. From the same Table, it could be noticed that the number of shops, showrooms visited significantly differs between the users and non-users of all the information sources. The difference is very high (more than 40 percent) in retail outlet source when the consumer visited one shop/showroom. This is also tested with chi-square test, the results of which are presented in Table 5.12, 13 and 14.

Table 5.11 : Frequency Distribution of Number of Shops Visited and Information Users and Non-Users (In Percentage)

Number of Shops Visited	*Personal Sources*		*Commercial Sources*		*Retail Outlet Sources*	
	Users	*Non-Users*	*Users*	*Non-Users*	*Users*	*Non-Users*
No answer	1.52	0.00	0.00	2.00	0.00	1.60
None	9.52	0.00	10.00	9.87	8.67	10.53
One	47.42	56.93	34.32	47.48	17.19	57.19
Two	7.59	22.32	19.32	9.43	29.68	3.42
More than two	33.95	20.75	36.36	31.22	44.46	27.26
Total	100.00	100.00	100.00	100.00	100.00	100.00

(**Source :** Primary Data).

Table 5.12 : Information Sources and Number of Shops, Dealers, Show Rooms Visited (Independent Test for Personal Sources)

Personal Sources	*Number of Shops Visited*					*Purchased from Private*
	No Answer	*None*	*One Shop*	*Two Shops*	*More than two shops*	
Users	20	231	649	121	412	74
Non-users	0	12	163	41	53	04
Total	20	243	812	162	465	78

Chi-Square Test

Degree of freedom	*Chi-square value*	*Table value @ 1% level*
5	62.3	15.09

(**Source :** Primary Data).

Table 5.13 : Information Sources and Number of Shops, Dealers, Show Rooms Visited (Independent Test for Commercial Sources)

Commercial Sources	*Number of Shops Visited*					*Purchased from Private*
	No Answer	*None*	*One Shop*	*Two Shops*	*More than two shops*	
Users	20	57	495	93	252	42
Non-users	0	186	317	69	213	36
Total	20	243	812	162	465	78

Chi-Square Test

Degree of freedom	*Chi-square value*	*Table value @ 1% level*
5	124.61	15.09

(**Source :** Primary Data).

It could be seen in this Table that the table value of x^2 at 1 percent level for d.f. 5 are 15.09. The computed value of x^2 for all personal, commercial, and retail outlet sources are

Table 5.14 : Information Sources and Number of Shops, Dealers, Show Rooms Visited (Independent Test for Retail Outlet Sources)

Retail outlet Sources	*Number of Shops Visited*					*Purchased from Private*
	No Answer	*None*	*One Shop*	*Two Shops*	*More than two shops*	
Users	20	56	294	98	123	16
Non-users	0	187	518	64	342	62
Total	20	243	812	162	465	78

Chi-Square Test

Degree of freedom	*Chi-square value*	*Table value @ 1% level*
5	122.24	15.09

(**Source :** Primary Data).

62.3, 124.61 and 122.24 respectively, which are higher than the table value confirming that there is significant difference between the users and non-users of the three information sources with reference to number of shops visited.

From the above analysis, it could be concluded that the maximum number of shops or showrooms visited by the sample consumers is one or two. Only the users of retail outlet source in the sample visited more than two shops. This number is dependent with relation to all the sources in the populations.

The Number of Brands Considered at the Time of Making the Final Choice

In the external search process, a consumer is engaged in collecting various information about the product, particularly about the number of brands of the product available in the market. If he has narrowed his mind after problem recognition to a particular brand, due to his past experience, he need not consider the other brands. But if he is in search of alternative brands, he collects more information from the market. Initially, a consumer usually considers more number of brands, but later on, at the time of making the purchase, he might have reduced the number of brands so that he can choose easily from the smaller number, by eliminating other brands due to several reasons of his own taste and preference. Though the consumer knows more number of brands available in the market, he may not consider all the brands at the time of making the final choice. The different sources of information definitely have influence on knowing about the market and on the final number of brands considered. An attempt is made here to find out the difference between users and non-users of the three sources of information in relation to number of brands considered at the time of making the final choice.

The frequency distribution of the number of brands considered and information sources used and not used by the population are summarized in Table 5.15. From the Table, it could be noticed that there is significant difference between the users and non-users, particularly the difference is very high when the number of brands considered is one (about 44 percent) in retail outlet source. It can also be

Table 5.15 : Frequency Distribution of Number of Brands Considered and Information Users and Non-Users (In Percentage)

Number of Brands	*Personal Sources*		*Commercial Sources*		*Retail Outlet Sources*	
	Users	*Non-Users*	*Users*	*Non-Users*	*Users*	*Non-Users*
No Answer	0.81	7.90	1.86	2.68	4.22	1.76
One Brand	34.72	36.27	38.79	48.00	8.03	52.18
Two Brands	46.13	12.89	30.46	31.96	46.92	30.06
Three Brands	6.40	9.00	5.81	3.84	19.98	5.93
More Than Three	11.94	33.94	23.08	13.52	20.85	10.07
Total	100.00	100.00	100.00	100.00	100.00	100.00

(**Source :** Primary Data).

inferred that among users more than 80 percent of personal source users, 69 percent of the commercial source users, and about 54 percent of the retail outlet source users considered only one or two brands at the time of making the final choice. The relationship has been verified by applying the chi-square test, the results of which are presented in Tables 5.16, 17 and 18.

Table 5.16 : Information Sources and Number of Brands Considered (Independent Test for Personal Sources)

	Number of Brands Considered				
Personal Sources	*No Answer*	*One Brand*	*Two Brands*	*Three Brands*	*More than Three Brands*
Users	15	624	440	73	194
Non- users	25	96	52	25	48
Total	40	720	492	98	242

Chi-Square Test

Degree of freedom	*Chi-square value*	*Table value @ 1% level*
4	90.2	13.28

(**Source** : Primary Data).

Table 5.17 : Information Sources and Number of Brands Considered (Independent Test for Commercial Sources)

	Number of Brands Considered				
Commercial Sources	*No Answer*	*One Brand*	*Two Brands*	*Three Brands*	*More than Three Brands*
Users	15	272	282	65	108
Non- users	25	448	210	33	134
Total	40	720	492	98	242

Chi-Square Test

Degree of freedom	*Chi-square value*	*Table value @ 1% level*
4	90.47	13.28

(**Source :** Primary Data).

Table 5.18 : Information Sources and Number of Brands Considered (Independent Test for Retail outlet Sources)

	Number of Brands Considered				
Retail outlet Sources	*No Answer*	*One Brand*	*Two Brands*	*Three Brands*	*More than Three Brands*
Users	15	23	180	42	93
Non- users	25	697	312	56	149
Total	40	720	492	98	242

Chi-Square Test

Degree of freedom	*Chi-square value*	*Table value @ 1% level*
4	259.6	13.28

(**Source :** Primary Data).

It could be seen in Tables 5.16, 17 and 18 that the table value of x^2 is 13.28 for d.f.4 at 1 per cent level which is lower than the computed values of all the three sources which are 90.2, 90.47 and 259.6 respectively, proving that there is significant difference in number of brands considered between user and non-user of all three sources of information.

From the above analysis, it could be concluded that the maximum number of brands considered is one or two in the samples, and it is a dependent variable, which relate to all the source of information in the sample.

Information Sources and Personal Characteristics

Consumers differ in many ways. It is possible to think of the various kinds of consumer characteristics as forming general-specific characteristics, running from demographic and socio-economic characteristics at one end to purchasing and consumption characteristics at the other. Some of the demographic characteristics are (a) age, (b) sex, (c) geographical location, (d) family life cycle etc. Some socio-economic characteristics are (a) occupation, (b) education, (c) income and (d) social class. So an attempt is made here to find out the relationship between information sources and the above-mentioned variables.

Age and Information Sources

The chi-square values of samples are given in Table 5.19. From the Table, it could be noticed that the calculated value of X^2 for personal, commercial, and retail outlet sources are 54.39, 23.62 and 21.95 respectively for the total population, which is greater than the table value 11.34, proving that age, and all the three information sources are dependent.

Table 5.19 : Test of Independent-Chi-Square Test

Variables	*Chi - Square Values*
Personal Sources and Age	54.39
Commercial Sources and Age	23.62
Retail Outlet Sources and Age	21.95

d. f. = 3; Table value @ 1% level = 11.34.

(**Source :** Primary Data).

So it could be concluded that age and information sources are dependent on each other in the total population.

Education and Information Sources

It is surprising to note that education and information sources in the population are independent. The calculated values of x^2 for all the information sources in the population are summarized in Table 5.20, in which it could be inferred that the calculated values are lower than the table value. It

Table 5.20 : Test of Independent -Chi-Square Test

Variables	*Chi - Square Values*
Personal Sources and Education	8.37
Commercial Sources and Education	3.46
Retail Outlet Sources and Education	0.67

d. f. = 3; Table value @ 1% level = 11.34.

(**Source :** Primary Data).

could be concluded that the information sources used or not used is in no way connected with education of the consumer.

Gender and Information Sources

The chi-square values of the sample for information sources and gender are summarized in Table 5.21. From the Table, it could be inferred that the calculated value of X^2 for personal source is 30.67, which is higher than the table value 9.21 proving that gender and personal sources are dependent. But on the other hand, the calculated value of X^2 for the other two sources in the sample are lower than the table value indicating that the two variables, gender and sources are independent.

Table 5.21 : Test of Independent -Chi-Square Test

Variables	*Chi - Square Values*
Personal Sources and Gender	30.67
Commercial Sources and Gender	9.06
Retail Outlet Sources and Gender	2.19
d. f. = 2; Table value @ 1% level = 9.21	

(**Source :** Primary Data).

Income and Information Sources

The chi-square values of the samples for the information sources and income are summarized in Table 5.22. It could be noticed that the calculated values for all the information sources in the samples are lower than the table value. It is

Table 5.22 : Test of Independent - Chi-Square Test

Variables	*Chi - Square Values*
Personal Sources and Income	6.33
Commercial Sources and Income	4.94
Retail Outlet Sources and Income	4.78
d. f. = 3; Table value @ 1% level = 11.34	

(**Source :** Primary Data).

indicating that the income and information sources are independent variables. In other words, it could be concluded that income level of the consumer has to do nothing with the information sources used/not used.

Occupation and Information Sources

Like education and income, occupation of the consumer also in no way connected with the information sources used / not used. This can be inferred from the Table 5.23, in which the chi-square values of the samples are summarized. It could be noticed that the X^2 values for all the information sources in the samples are lower than the table value indicating that the two variables, occupation and information sources are independent.

Table 5.23 : Test of Independent -Chi-Square Test

Variables	*Chi - Square Values*
Personal Sources and Occupation	12.04
Commercial Sources and Occupation	4.92
Retail Outlet Sources and Occupation	13.07
d. f. = 12; Table value @ 1% level =26.22	

(**Source :** Primary Data).

Section Summary

The following conclusions could be drawn from the discussion in this section.

(i) The total consumers considered commercial source as the most important source, both from the viewpoint of exposure and effectiveness.

(ii) In analyzing the time taken by the sample population (i.e. time lag between contemplation and actual purchase) personal source users and retail outlet source users took one to four weeks only, while the users of the commercial sources, took more than four weeks. At the time of finding out the relationship between these two factors (time taken and information sources) time taken is acting, as an independent factor in relation to personal source while it is a dependent factor in relation to the other two sources.

(iii) While analyzing the level of planning, all the users of three information sources in the sample population have planned carefully for their purchases. In finding out the relationship between level of planning and the three information sources, in the total population, the level of planning is considered as a dependent factor, relative to all the information sources.

(iv) The number of shops, showrooms visited by the sample population is one or two only. The percentage is equal in retail outlet source users among the sample population where they also visited more than two shops. In bringing out the relationship between the number of shops visited and the three information sources, it could be concluded that the variables are dependent on each other in the samples.

(v) The majority of the users of all the sources of information in the total sample population considered only one or two brands at the time of making the final choice. In bringing out the relationships between the number of brands considered and the three information sources, for the population, the former is considered to be a dependent factor in relation to the latter.

(vi) Generally speaking, demographic and socio-economic characteristics, which are selected for the study, are acting as an independent variables relative to information sources. There are some exceptions also, where all the sources and age, and personal source and sex are dependent in the sample.

EVALUATIVE CRITERIA IN PURCHASE DECISIONS

In almost every product, there are a number of alternatives for a consumer; be it a day to day consumer product like grocery, butter, bread, tea, coffee, or consumer durables like television's, refrigerators, air conditioners, motor bikes, scooters, cars, houses, insurance policies, courier and other services. In India, till the processes of liberalization started in 1991, consumer had very little choice, and he had to buy what was offered to him. For instance, before Maruthi Udyog started producing cars, there were only three models in India, and they were also in short supply. Hence, one had to buy what was offered to him. Today, there are over 30 models, and more are introduced now and then. Hence consumer can decide which one is the best alternative for him. Similarly, in the case of televisions, refrigerators, air conditioners, washing machines and other products a number of alternatives are available, and the consumer has to make a choice out of them, after assessing their relative merits and demerits. Thus, "alternative evaluation can be defined as the process by which a choice alternative is evaluated and selected to meet consumer needs". In other words, it is the study of processes by which consumer makes a final choice to buy a particular brand of bread, butter, cheese, tea, coffee, milk, car or other consumer durables or services. The consumer studies various factors to help him to evaluate. For instance, in the case of car, he considers price, fuel consumption, durability, and reputation of manufacture, besides colour and shape. The selection of costly durable items is done with great care; one collects the information on various models available. Then he eliminates those, which are beyond his budget. In the next stage, he shortlists two / three models, and studies them in depth for which he may consult his friends, relatives, and those who have some technical knowledge about the product, and finally he selects one model[4] as given in the chart below. The number of stages for selection differs from product to product, and for some items like property, insurance even the help of consultants is taken. In the case of items of daily use, choice is very simple, and often it is made on the basis of past experience and short memory. Some of these products are also purchased on recommendations of retailers or friends or influenced by advertisements. However, in the case of high value items, which have, long life, and one has to live with them for years together, the consumer is very careful in selection because he has to incur loss if wrong choice is made.

The process of evaluation undergoes several stages, which are presented in Fig.5.3 below:

Fig. 5.3 Process of Alternative Evaluation

Process of Alternative Evaluation

↓

Decide the Product to be Purchased

↓

Gather Information on Alternative Brands Available in the Market

↓

Determine the Criteria for Evaluation

↓

Take a Final Decision on Brand, Based on Determinative Criteria

Criteria for Evaluation

Once a consumer feels the necessity of evaluating a product, he decides the criterion or criteria to be used. The important of them are as under:

- Price
- Brand i.e. reputation of manufacture
- Attributes of the product
- Experience-his own or that of relatives and friends
- Familiarity
- Trade off between positive and negative effects
- The number of alternatives to be considered
- Product recognition for familiarity, based criteria for decision in the consideration set.

- Name recognition
- Advertisement
- Accessibility
- Usage
- Memory
- Objectives of purchase
- Quality evaluation
- Beliefs
- Performance
- Cost of use i.e. running cost of various alternatives
- Life of the product
- Efficiency, especially in case of service
- Country of origin
- Consistency
- Features
- Innovative technology
- Trial
- Reliance
- After-sales service

The above list is only an illustrative criterion, which a consumer may like to consider in evaluating a product or service. It is not necessary to consider all of them for each product. Further, consumer may choose other criteria, which he feels appropriate, based on his knowledge, information, and family influence for a particular product or service. He may also decide to get an opinion of experts in high value, long life products or service like house property, car, computer system, insurance policy etc, and may decide to base his decision entirely on project report or evaluation which these days appear in newspapers, magazines, special journals etc. In such a case, he may have criteria for use of these studies and opinion to check his own decision to arrive at a final decision.

In the evaluation process, the consumer is able to analyse the information, obtained in the search process, and make a final decision regarding the purchase.

Evaluate or Choice Criteria

Choice criteria refer to the standards and specifications the consumers' uses in evaluating products and brands of their objective or subjective choice[5]. It may vary from one or more evaluative criteria for high involvement products than for low involvement ones; and that the number of evaluative criteria is fewer or as high as nine[6].

Reducing the Range of Alternatives

Sometimes, the consumer will not be able to choose from the alternatives he is aware of, for various reasons. Some of the brands may be beyond his financial reach; some may not suit his motives; some may not be evaluated for lack of sufficient information (inter set); some may have tried and rejected; some may be dissatisfactory; and some other due to negative feed back from advertising or oral communication (inter set)[7].

Evaluating Alternatives

The consumer usually tries to evaluate brands either by Brand Processing Method (BPM) or Attribute Processing Method (APM). In the former method, brands are compared one by one, and in the later one, attribute of the particular brand is compared with that of another brand and so on and so forth. While BPM is common, APM is not uncommon in the early stages as research shows [8].

Factors Influencing the Amount of Evaluation

Though there are so many factors, influencing the amount of evaluation, it will be less depending upon the urgency of the need, and more depending upon the significance of the product and the complexity of the alternatives. Hence, based on this, the consumer may get the desire to buy a product but there is a time gap between the desire to buy and actual purchase.

Time Gap Between Intention and Actual Purchase

When a person gets a desire or intention to buy a durable product, it may not materialize soon in the form of actual purchase. The purchase may take its own time. All of our desires are not fulfilled, and if at all they are fulfilled, it may not necessarily be immediately. This aspect of consumer behaviour will be of much interest to marketers for converting the desire into purchase by following suitable marketing strategies. In this regard, the opinions of the 450 respondents were sought by asking them to reveal the time gap between the intention to buy and the actual purchase.

Evaluation criteria, of course, are expressed in terms of desired product attributes. Some of the more common attributes which are used in this study are price (equal and chapter), appearance, style, colour etc., brand popularity, service and spare-parts, technical performance, special discount, easy installment, availability of product, participation in prize contest, gift, easy operation, dealer location, and reputation and warranty.

Factor Analysis

In order to ascertain key factors, determining purchase decision, factor-analysis is employed. Factor analysis is a generic name given to a class of techniques whose purpose often consists of data reduction and summarization. Used in this way, the objective is to represent a set of observed variables (or persons or occasions) in terms of a smaller number of hypothetical, underlying and unknown dimensions, which are called factors. This type of factor analysis is the most common type used in marketing research applications. There are common factors that have effects shared in common with more than one of the observed variables and unique factors in which effects are shared with only one observed variables.

Factor analysis is a method for determining the number and nature of the underlying variables among larger number of measures. More succinctly, it is a method for determining 'k' underlying variables (factors) from 'n' sets of measures, 'k' being less than 'n'. It may also be called a method for extracting common factor variances from sets of measures[9].

Methods of Factor Analysis

There are a number of methods of factor analysis-correlation matrix: principal factors, centroid, diagonal, maximum likelihood, multiple group, minres, image, alpha and so on. We cannot discuss all these methods. Therefore, we describe the method that is used the most at present, and that is widely available at computer installations: the principal factors method.

The reader may ask: why not use a comparatively simple cluster method like the inspection approach used earlier, instead of a complex method like the Principal Factors Method?. Cluster Methods can be used and have been recommended. They depend upon our identifying clusters and presumed factors by findings interrelated groups of correlation coefficients or other measures of relation, the clusters are easy to find. In most 'R' matrices, however, the clusters cannot be so easily identified. More objectives and precise methods are needed.

The Principal Factor Method

The Principal Factors Method is mathematically satisfying because it yields a mathematically unique solution of a factor problem. Perhaps its major solution feature is that it extracts a maximum amount of variance as each factor is calculated. In other words, the first factor extracts the most variance, the second, the next most variance, and so on.

To show the logic of the Principal Factors Method without considerable mathematics is difficult. One can achieve a certain intuitive understanding of the method, however, by approaching it geometrically. Conceive tests or variables as points in m-dimensional space. Variables that are highly and positively correlated should be near each other and away from variables with which they do not correlate. If this reasoning is correct, there should be swarms of points in space. Each of these points can be located in the space if suitable axes are inserted into the space, one axis for each dimension of the 'm' dimensions. Then any point's location is its multiple identification obtained by reading its coordinates on the 'm' axes.

The factor problem is to shoot axes through neighbouring swarms of points and to so locate these axes that they "account for" as much of the variances of the variables as possible.

Factors analysis is used to find out different groups of attributes which are considered as important in taking a purchase decision of four products: television, refrigerator, air cooler, washing machine among the consumers. The Principal Component Analysis finds linear combinations of attributes, explaining the variability, contributed by individual variables. These linear combinations can be further studied to find individual variables, giving rise to variation of large order. The principal components are nothing but the eigen vectors of the variance-covariance matrix. From this, the eigen values are computed and the corresponding principal components are arrived at. Once the principal components have been derived, factor analysis has been carried out to group the variables.

TELEVISION: FACTOR STRUCTURE FOR CONSUMERS

Television, in India has already become a much-wanted consumer "product" in the study areas. Although it is often looked upon as an entertainment medium for several people, it has become a daily habit. The spread of television, or rather the use of it, however, has been slow.

Looked at from the point of view of consumers, as can be seen from the other factor structure matrix, the relative position of the variables chosen for analysis becomes clear.

Cumulative Percentage of Variance

In the factor structure for consumers, seven factors have been extracted. The factors extracted for the consumer's case explain a total variance of 58.53 per cent, although in only five of the factors, the eigen value is more than 1.0. If it has been according to the findings of the factor analysis, with regard to extraction of factors, the factors with eigen values of more than 1.0 have to be extracted, and so only five factors in consumer cases have been studied[10]. Since the factors which have eigen values less than 1.0 are not given much importance, and hence are not taken into account for interpretation purpose in this study. The cumulative percentage of variance and percentage of variance accounted for each factor with eigen values of television are summarized in Table 5.24.

Table 5.24 : Cumulative Percentage of Variance and Percentage of Variance Accounted for by Each Factor with Eigen Values Television

Factors	*Titles*	*% of Variance Accounted for by Each Factor*	*Cumulative % of Variance*	*Eigen Values*
1.	Installment and Price	20.17	20.17	3.121
2.	Price, Model and Discount	13.82	33.99	1.671
3.	Warranty, Installment and Price	10.36	44.35	1.439
4.	Price and Gift	7.45	51.80	1.162
5.	Prize, price and Dealer attributes	6.73	58.53	1.123

Installment and Pricing

The first factor, "Installment and Pricing", is the main dimension. And hence the variables with high loadings here are in effect the dominant variables determining, rather indirectly but nevertheless, the consumer behaviour of the people in the study area. This factor accounts for 20.17 percent of the total variance and has an eigen value of 3.121. It is observed from the loadings on the four variables listed in the Table 5.25 that easy installment is the most important of the variables with high significant loadings. The loading

Table 5.25 : Factor Structure-Television (0.4 Cut-off for Significant Loading)

Factors / Titles	*Variables*	*Loadings*
1. Installment and Price	Easy installment	0.692
	cheaper price	0.621
	equal price	0.542
	dealer location	-0.421
2. Price, Model and Discount	cheaper price	0.676
	appearance, style, colour	0.672
	special discount	0.422
	dealer reputation	-0.761
	availability of product	-0.793
3. Warranty, Installment and Price	warranty	0.731
	easy installments	0.623
	equal price	0.541
	appearance, style, colour	0.476
	easy to operate	0.459
	dealer location	0.401
4. Price and Gift	special gift	0.646
	equal price	0.509
	cheaper price	0.421
	availability of product	-0.617
	prize contest	-0.401
	warranty	-0.419
5. Prize, Price and Dealer attributes	prize contest	0.612
	dealer location	0.582
	equal price	0.538
	dealer reputation	0.512
	technical performance	0.508

(**Source :** Primary Data).

as well as the variables' position is understandable from the viewpoint of consumers, as most television buyers are middle-income salaried people. And installment, or what is popularly known-although a misnomer-as 'hire purchase' is the dominant mode of purchase. The reason for this is not far to seek; most of these households are able to make such purchases only by making a provision in the monthly household budget.

But in the purchases, even under an installment system the consumers prefer cheaper prices, and also look for equal prices (relative to other brands of goods-television here), and hence the two variables get high loadings and positive at that. Dealer location is, however, negatively loaded, and it is perhaps because dealers are a few and far between, and hence people may have to look for dealers elsewhere who are close by. The eigen values on dealer location does indicate that it is relevant, and it is included in the first dimension, but it would be whether it is close by or far away for competitive buying is important.

Price, Model, Discount

The second factor given in the Table 5.25 is designated as "Price Model and Discount", based on positively loaded variables, explaining a variance of 13.82 per cent, and has an eigen value of 1.671. This is the bipolar, and hence the five variables listed under it are important. The data set through factor loadings that for television buyers, model qualities (in terms of appearance, style, colour, etc., because these are the attractive attributes of the 'good' buy), and discount are as important as installment and pricing in the first factor.

However, dealer reputation as a variable gets a high negative loading because in purchases, dealer reputation is not always looked into or if it is, it is not a very important consideration in most cases. Again, availability of product or preferred brand gets a high negative loading. It can be explained from the fact that there are several dealers in the cities, and the product is available with most of the dealers, and consumers can choose the brand or model they wish to buy.

Warranty, Installments and Price

The third factor, in the Table 5.25 labelled "Warranty, Installment and Price", indicated rather very succinctly the importance given by the buyers to warranty. The period of warranty gives a sense of security to the consumer, and probably tells about the confidence, which the manufacturer has on the unfailing service of the product. The fact that this factor has the variables found in factors one and two and with high significant and positive loadings reinforce the importance of installment 0.623, price 0.541, model qualities 0.476 as variables affecting consumer behaviour, although it is a reduced dimension. Ease of operation here gets a positive loading 0.459, and dealer location 0.401 is included in it with significant positive loading. It means they are relatively important in determining the consumer behaviour vis-à-vis television purchases. This factor has a total variance of 10.36 per cent and an eigen value of 1.439.

Price and Gift

From the Table 5.25, it could be noticed that the repeated occurrence of prices (equal and cheaper) in the first three, as well as in this fourth factor, labelled "Price and Gift", further reinforces the value of price in consumer behaviour. Television as special gifts (for special gifts as a variable is highly loaded with0.646) is something very important in the factor, for this shows a typical facet of purchases, and thus of consumer behaviour. It should however be construed as part of 'savings and purchase' scheme that are afloat in the cities. The special gifts are therefore an inducement that dealers must provide for more savings and more purchases by the consumer. This is made clear by low loadings and negative on variables such as prize contest (-401) and warranty (-0.419). This factor explains a variance to the total of 7.45 per cent and has eigen value of 1.162.

Prize, Price and Dealer Attributes

From the Table 5.25, it could be noticed that the fifth factor has five variables with high, significant and all positive loadings and could be labelled as the "Prize, Price and Dealer Attributes". The variables that have been loaded either low or negative in the earlier factors get high, and positive loadings make them now relevant in the total factor structure. In particular, prize contest (0.612), dealer location

(0.582), dealer reputation (0.512) and technical performance all with positive loadings indicate that in the context of consumer behaviour, these variables as factors influencing are far removed from the main dimension. They are nevertheless important and therefore included in the fifth factor with an eigen value of 1.123 and a variance of 6.73 per cent.

Inter-Correlation Matrix for the Consumers of Televisions

From the Inter- correlation matrix given in Table 5.26 only two pairs of variables in the entire set of 15 variables show statistically significant relations. They are equal price and special discount with r = 0.475 and model and brand popularity with r = 0.412. All other relevant relationships are either low correlations or statistically insignificant, although there are some 'spurious correlations' too.

Table 5.26 : Inter-Correlation Matrix Television

Sl. No.	*Variables*	*'r'*
1.	Equal price and special discount	0.475
2.	Model and brand popularity	0.412

As in the entire case, prices repeatedly occur with varying loadings with the both positive and negative signs in the factors extracted, perhaps explaining the very importance of price as a mechanism determining consumer performance.

REFRIGERATOR : FACTOR STRUCTURE FOR CONSUMERS

Cumulative Percentage of Variance

The factor structure of refrigerator consumers is quite different from that of television consumer's cases above. From Table 5.27 it could be seen that eight factors were extracted in the factor analysis of refrigerator consumer data, out of which only six factors have eigen values of more than 1.0. The six factors together explain a variance of a little more than 60 percent. The difference in the structure and therefore dimensional nuances of refrigerator consumer vis-à-vis television consumers are evident in the labels of factors extracted for the purpose of interpretation.

Table 5.27 : Cumulative Percentage of Variance and Percentage of Variance Accounted for by Each Factor with Eigen ValuesRefrigerator

Factors	*Titles*	*% of Variance Accounted for by Each Factor*	*Cumulative % of Variance*	*Eigen Values*
1.	Service, Prize and Mode	16.4311	16.431	2.692
2.	Price	11.807	28.238	1.751
3.	Warranty and Price	9.532	37.770	1.293
4.	Operational Ease and Price	7.965	45.735	1.192
5.	Dealer attributes and price	6.947	52.682	1.148
6.	Performance, Dealer Attributes and Discount	6.796	59.478	1.016

Service, Prize and Model

The main dimension, in Table 5.28 explains 16.4 per cent of the total variance with an eigen value of 2.692. Unlike those of the cases of television consumers has "Service, Prize and Model" as the dominant variables. Dealer reputation in this dimension gets a low negative loading, although the very same variable receives a low positive in the reduced fifth dimension. For refrigerator buyers, it is conspicuous that service and spare parts (0.904) and model qualities (0.443) matter much more than other variables. However, it is also indicated that many have acquired refrigerators through prize contests, held by hire purchase dealers, as this variable gets a high positive loading of (0.625).

Price

The bipolar factor which could be seen in the same Table has five variables with high loadings, but four of them negative, while only 'cheaper price' is with positive loading (0.442), and hence this factor is labelled "Price" even while it has been understood that the negatively loaded variables-brand popularity (-0.763), special discount (-0.619), availability of the product (-0.481), and dealer location (-0.449) alone should determine the strength of the factor. This factor accounts for 11.8 percent of total variance and has an eigen value of 1.751.

Table- 5.28 : Factor Structure-Refrigerator (0.4 Cut-off for Significant Loading)

Factors / Titles	*Variables*	*Loadings*
1. Service, Prize and Model	service and spare part	0.904
	prize contest	0.625
	appearance, style, colour	0.443
	dealer reputation	-0.461
2. Price	cheaper price	0.442
	brand popularity	-0.763
	special discount	-0.619
	availability of product	-0.481
	dealer location	-0.449
3. Warranty and Price	warranty	0.896
	equal price	0.512
4. Operational Ease and price	easy operation	0.562
	equal price	0.413
	technical performance	-0.512
	dealer reputation	-0.457
	warranty	-0.422
5. Dealer attributes and price	dealer reputation	0.549
	equal price	0.461
	dealerlocation	0.446
	special gift	-0.576
6. Performance, Dealer Attributes and Discount	technical performance	0.536
	dealer location	0.413
	discount	0.419

Warranty and Price

The third factor is clear-cut, with two variables, having positive loadings. And they are warranty (0.896) and equal price (0.512). This factor, which accounts for 9.53 per cent of variance, clearly indicated that refrigerator buyers, because the investment is high, are concerned with warranty, being offered on purchase, while at the same time, they are also particularly concerned about competitive prices.

Operational Ease and Price

The fourth factor is titled "Operational Ease and Price" with five variables having significant factor loadings, three negative and two positive. The fourth factor emphasizes rather upon the operational ease (0.562), which most refrigerators represent to a good measure. Anyway equal price (0.413), the variable more significantly loaded than here in the fourth factor, stresses the importance of competitive price in the purchase of refrigerators.

The other three variables, technical performance (-0.512) dealer reputation (-0.457) and warranty (-0.422) all get negative loadings. Together, these constituents explain a total variance of 7.97 per cent and have an eigen value of 1.192.

Dealer Attributes and Price

Dealer reputation (0.549), equal price (0.461) and dealer location (0.446) all get positive loadings and special gifts (-0.576) gets a negative loading being the fifth factor. The factor is labelled as "Dealer Attributes and Price" and accounts for a variance of 6.95 per cent. This factor is indicative of the fact that refrigerator buyers are affected by the reputation and location of dealers vis-à-vis their own location and equal price. Dealer location however gets a still higher loading in factor five.

Performance, Dealer Attributes and Discount

Included in the sixth, which is given in the Table 5.54 along with the technical performance (0.536), and special discount (0.419), and dealer location (0.413). Noticeably, the three variables are significantly positively loaded. A few words about special discount in order. In such purchases as that of television and refrigerator incurring high amounts of money, special discount is an offer normally associated with 'cash down' purchases. Sometimes, however, off-season offers of discount is encountered in sales of refrigerators and air cooler (in winter months). Also dealers while a publicity campaign may implement such offers of discount for the product is on.

Inter-Correlation Matrix for the Consumers of Refrigerator

Surprisingly, Inter-Correlation Matrix does not contain any pair of variables with the significant 0.400 coefficient, the cut off point taken for explaining for relationship in all these cases, except for one single pair-appearance, style, colour etc., and service and spare parts with high significant co-efficient of 0.412 although the relationship could be considered as 'spurious'.

AIR-COOLER-FACTOR STRUCTURE FOR CONSUMERS

Cumulative Percentage of Variance

Air-Cooler is a consumer product in common use at homes. Consumer behaviour as gleaned from the factor structure, present yet another factor of purchase decisions, quite different from those of the consumer behaviour in the case of television and refrigerator. Seven factors were extracted from the factor analysis of consumer data from the study area, out of which only five factors are explained here having eigen values of more than 1.0. These factors together account for a variance to the total of 60.964 per cent, which could be seen in Table 5.29.

Operational Ease, Prize and Service

The first factor is given in the Table 5.30, and is labelled "Operational Ease, Prize and Service". It speaks of the importance of the three variables in purchase decisions, although there are some other variables listed under it with high positive or negative loadings. Significantly in this factor, nine of the fifteen variables show up significant positive or negative loadings. The very high positive loading that the

Table 5.29 : Cumulative Percentage of Variance and Percentage of Variance Accounted for by Each Factor with Eigen Values Air Cooler

Factors	*Titles*	*% of Variance Accounted for by Each Factor*	*Cumulative % of Variance*	*Eigen Values*
1.	Operational Ease, Prize and Service	20.179	20.179	2.768
2.	Dealer Attributes and Easy Operation	11.959	32.138	1.943
3.	Price and Installment	10.986	43.124	1.642
4.	Dealer Attributes and Price	9.498	52.622	1.419
5.	Dealer Attributes, Service and Price	8.342	60.964	1.173

variable 'easy to operate' receives is understandable in that most of the houses that work with them to ease their chores at home look for such ease. Hence, decidedly, the high loading.

The high loading on prize contest as a variable is explainable in terms of contests held as a part as a marketing strategy by the dealers who more of them not go for attributes prize schemes, which undoubtedly boost their sales. Because, it is a common-use gadget, the consumers look for good services and equal price and for spare parts, and hence this variable is also highly loaded in the factor. In much the same way, the nine variables in the factor could be explained as to their relevance's in the main dimensions, with or without positive loadings. This factor explains a variance of 20.18 percent of the total, and has an eigen value of 2.768.

Dealer Attributes and Easy Operation

The two variables with significant positive loadings in the bipolar are the dealer location and operation ease. Thus the importance of operational ease made explicit in the

Table 5.30 : Factor Structure-Air Cooler (0.4 Cut-off for Significant Loading)

Factors / Titles	*Variables*	*Loadings*
1. Operational Ease, prize and Service	easy operation	0.918
	prize contest	0.817
	service and spare parts	0.742
	equal price	0.541
	brand popularity	-0.619
	appearance, style, colour, etc	-0.543
	cheaper price	-0.491
	special gift	-0.457
	dealer reputation	-0.419
2. Dealer Attributes and Easy Operation	dealer location	0.719
	easy operation	0.616
3. Price and Installment	equal price	0.573
	easy installment	0.562
	dealer location	-0.618
	prize contest	-0.576
4. Dealer Attributes and Price	dealer reputation	0.715
	equal price	0.518
	prize contest	0.416
	dealer location	0.469
5. Dealer attributes, service and price	dealer reputation	0.768
	service and spare parts	0.419
	equal price	0.475

bipolar also. The variance of this factor explains 12 percent and has an eign value of 1.943.

Price and Installment

The third factor explaining a variance of 11 per cent, consists of four variables with significant loadings, two positive and two negative. Installment is important in the case of air cooler consumer in the study area only in the reduced dimension. This, along with equal price, because there are competitive products of certain qualities available in the market, makeup the positive sides of the first of the reduced dimension extracted from the factor analysis. Dealer location and prize contest however receive negative loadings, which play down the role of these in the reduced dimension.

Dealer Attributes and Price

Dealer reputation (0.715), equal price (0.518), prize contest (0.416) and dealer location (0.469) all get positive loadings being the fourth factor. The factor is labelled as "Dealer Attributes and Price" and accounts for a variance of 9.5 percent. This factor is indicative of the fact that air-cooler buyers are affected by the reputation and location of dealers vis-à-vis their own location, equal price and prize contest.

Dealer Attributes, Service and Price

Included in the fifth factor, which is given in the Table 5.30 along with the dealer reputation (0.768), service and spare parts (0.419) and equal price (0.475). Noticeably, the three variables are significantly positively loaded. The fifth factor explains a variance of 8.34 per cent.

Dealer reputation, which the consumers indicated as one of the very important of all variables in the earlier factors occur with high positive loadings in both the fourth and the fifth factors as if the dimensions reinforce the value of it in the entire factor structure. Dealer location however gets a low positive loading in the fourth, and services and spare parts in the fifth.

Inter-Correlation Matrix for the Consumers of Air-cooler

Relation-wise, the two pairs of variables that have significant correlation coefficients are those of model and brand popularity and brand popularity and services and spare parts, which could be seen in Table 5.31. It could be safely said that people not only look for model qualities (appearance, style, colour etc.,) but also for popular brands: and not only popular brands but also for services and spare parts. Hence the relationships, the inter-correlation matrix indicate, are relevant for the analysis.

Table 5.31 : Inter-Correlation Matrix Air Cooler

Sl. No.	*Variables*	*'r'*
1.	Model and Brand	0.419
2.	Brand and Service and Spare Parts	0.426

WASHING MACHINE: FACTOR STRUCTURES FOR CONSUMERS

Cumulative Percentage of Variance

Washing machine has been in great use in the study areas. The price level, product features, and price range for this product are such that the preference for this product could be assumed to be nearly the same for buyers. Hence, the data on the consumers have been used for factor analysis to extract a total of six factors. However, only the first five have an eigen value more than 1.0, while the sixth has less than one. Together, the factors have accounted for a total variance of 63.77, as is seen in Table 5.32.

Tabel 5.32 : Cumulative Percentage of Variance and Percentage of Variance Accounted for by Each Factor with Eigen Values Washing Machine

Factors	*Titles*	*% of Variance Accounted for by Each Factor*	*Cumulative % of Variance*	*Eigen Values*
1.	Warranty and Dealer Attributes	21.017	21.017	3.179
2.	Discount and Dealer Attributes	17.961	38.978	2.842
3.	Price and Availability	11.419	50.397	1.986
4.	Price performance and Dealer Attributes	7.342	57.739	1.482
5.	Gift and Prize	6.027	63.766	1.092

Warranty and Dealer Attributes

Washing machine is more ubiquitous (than television, refrigerator and Air cooler) and hence naturally throw up a different factor structure altogether. The main dimension, which is given in Table 5.33, consists of warranty (0.812) and dealer location (0.518) with high and significant loadings in the positive while the availability of service spare parts (-0.622) and prize consult (-0.761) receive statistically

Table-5.33 : Factor Structure-Washing Machine (0.4 Cut-off for Significant Loading)

Factors / Titles	*Variables*	*Loadings*
1. Warranty and Dealer Attributes	warranty	0.812
	dealer location	0.518
	prize contest	-0.761
	service and spare parts	-0.622
2. Discount and Dealer Attributes	special discount	0.598
	dealer reputation	0.401
	easy operation	-0.998
	service and spare parts	-0.943
	dealer location	-0.846
	equal price	-0.819
	warranty	-0.529
3. Price and Availability	cheaper price	0.617
	availability of product	0.612
	equal price	0.571
	special discount	0.562
	special gift	0.512
	dealer location	-0.817
	dealer reputation	-0.818
4. Price, performance and Dealer Attributes	dealer location	0.492
	cheaper price	0.491
	technical performance	0.428
	easy installment	-0.830
	prize contest	-0.812
	appearance, style, colour	-0.553
	easy operation	-0.461
5. Gift and prize	special gift	0.773
	prize contest	0.598
	easy installment	0.452
	warranty	0.411
	availability of product	-0.430

significant negative loadings. It must be remembered that in the case of washing machine for which the price itself is comparatively high; the price range between different models, and brands is also comparatively broad; the product features (colour, appearance, size etc.,) being more or less similar, the consumer moves to other criteria for evaluation. Thus, it appears warranty, which may vary from a few months to a few years, and dealer location, which perhaps is in good number; take the lead in purchase decisions of washing machine. While this factor explains a variance of 21.017 percent.

Discount and Dealer Attributes

In terms of bipolar, it should be mentioned with respect to positively loaded variables that being a product of high cost, most people buy with special discount, and hence special discount can weigh much in their purchase decisions. Also dealer reputation, to a certain extent, makes for faster decisions. The bipolar explains a variance of 18 percent with only special discount and dealer reputation with positive loadings and other with negative loadings.

Price and Availability

The third factor, which is labelled 'Price and Availability' in fact, has several variables with significant positive loadings, and they are, cheaper price (0.617) availability of product (0.612), equal price (0.571) special discount (0.562) and special gift (0.512). These variables need no explanation in that they continue to appear in factors extracted not only in the case discussed now but also in others as well. The third factor has dealer location and dealer reputation with high negative loadings, and these have however received positive loadings in the main and the bipolar.

Price, Performance and Dealer Attributes

The fourth factor is a factor of 'Price, Performance and Dealer Attributes', although listed under it are the variables such as those of dealer location, cheaper price, and technical performance with high positive loadings. The variance for the factor is 7.342 percent.

Gifts and Prizes

The fifth factor is of 'Gifts and Prizes' with the two variables very highly positively loaded, and also included in it are the variables of easy installment and warranty. This factor accounts for a variance of 6.027 percent.

Inter-Correlation Matrix for the Consumer of Washing Machine

In this analysis, relationships are statistically significant between a number of pairs of variables, and such pairs are those of the equal price and cheaper price, equal price and model qualities, price and installments, price and discount, service and spare parts and dealer location, and special discount and easy installment, which are given in Table 5.34.

Table 5.34: Inter-Correlation Matrix Washing Machine

Sl. No.	*Variables*	*'r'*
1.	Equal price and cheaper price	0.576
2.	Equal price and model	0.441
3.	Equal price and easy installment	0.521
4.	Cheaper price and special discount	0.515
5.	Cheaper price and easy installment	0.583
6.	Service and spare parts and dealer location	0.407
7.	Special discount and easy installment	0.732

Section Summary

The fifteen variables selected for evaluative criteria are reduced into different groups of 'Factors'. Even though, more than five or six factors are extracted in each case for the purpose of analysis, only the first two factors i.e., the First Factor (main dimension), and the Second Factor (bipolar) are taken into account for the purpose of the present summary and overall conclusions.

One most striking feature of the factor structures is that 'price' finds a place in all the three products, which means that this economic consideration is much relevant. Further, most of the other variables (installment, discount, prize, gift) found within these factor structures also make economic sense. Thus, as far as these products are concerned, the evaluative criteria appear to be mainly 'economic' or 'utility' oriented rather than 'psychological' (status, prestige, aesthetic sense).

With respect to the fourth product, viz., (washing machine) the Two Factors have been extracted on the first.

The washing machine being the modest in the market has a more or less 'settled price' and with only marginal product variation possible for price differentiation, the consumer perceptions focus on the other factors which include warranty, easy installment and special discount on the 'settled price'.

Collectively speaking, the factor analysis in all cases has shown consistently the relevance of some variables and such variables, in some order of importance, are those of price, availability, discount, easy installment, dealer location and reputation, operational ease, technical performance and services and spare parts. Operational ease also weighed heavily, more especially, with product like air-cooler rather than that of television, refrigerator and washing machine. The purchase decisions, it would appear from the inferences made, depend more on economic variables rather than on preference like model features, although these features are not lost sight of by the consumers in the case of television, which are a status as well as a decorative product.

REFERENCES AND NOTES

1. Frederic May, (1982), "An Appraisal of Buying Behaviour Research", ed., Peter R.Bennett, Marketing and Economic Development. P.397 as indicated in James Engel and Roger D. Blackwell, "Consumer Behaviour", Holt-Saunders International Editions, The Dryden Press, p.334.

2. Ibid. p. 334.
3. Engel and Blackwell, op. cit., p. 26.
4. P.C. Jain and Monika Bhatt, (2003), "Consumer Behaviour", in Indian Context, S. Chand, New Delhi, p. 173.
5. John A.Howard, (1977), "Consumer Behaviour: Application of Theory", McGraw Hill, New York, p. 29.
6. James F.Engel and Roger D. Blackwell, (1982), "Consumer Behaviour", New York: Dryden Press, (4th ed.), p. 418.
7. Chern L.Narayana and Rorn J. Markein, (1975), "Consumer Behaviour and Product Performance: An Alternative Conceptualization", *Journal of Marketing,* (October), Vol. 39 (2).
8. James R.Bettman and Park C. Whan, (1980), "Effects of Prior Knowledge and Experience and Phase of the Choice Process on Consumer Decision Process: A Protocol Analysis", *Journal of Consumer Research,* Vol. 77, pp. 234-284.
9. G.Thomoson, (1951), "The Factorial Analysis of Human Ability", Boston: Houghton-Mifflin, Chap, VII, p. 667.
10. Peter Gould, (1966), "On Interpreting Eigen Values in Factor Analysis", Transactions of Institute of Geographers, pp. 53-83.

6

Factors Influencing the Consumers in the Decision Making Process

The objective of this chapter is to present the factors that influence the consumers in the purchase of four selected consumer durable products. After the consumer has decided the criteria to be considered, he evaluates various alternatives and then makes a choice between different products. In this process, he is influenced by motivation.

CONSUMER MOTIVATION

Motivation plays an important role in the lives of people, especially consumers, for; it is almost impossible for a consumer to buy anything sans motivation. Psychologists and consumer behaviourists agree that basically most people experience the same kinds of needs and motives, and it is these motives, which find expression in various ways. Modern marketing is consumer-oriented, directed towards satisfaction of consumers, which require a thorough understanding of their buying motives.

Motivation is the driving force within individuals that impels them to action.[1] Motives are those influences or considerations, which provide the impulse to buy, to induce action or determine choice in the purchase of goods or services. The following model (fig. 6.1) explains the motivation process:-

Fig. 6.1 : Model of the Motivation Process

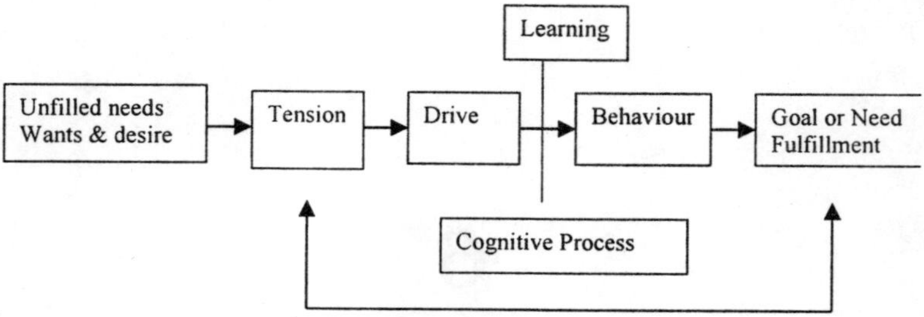

The motivational process consists in either conscious or sub-conscious consumer behaviour, which strives to fulfil and an unfulfilled need, and thereby release the tension.[2]

Goals are sought-after results of motivated behaviour. All behaviour is goal-oriented. Needs and goals are inter-dependent; one does not exist without the other. The goals selected by individuals depend on their personal experiences, physical capacity, prevailing cultural norms and values, and the goals accessibility in the physical social environment. Human needs and motives are inextricably linked; the relationship between them is very close that it becomes extremely difficult to identify the precise difference, which may characterize them. According to Baytor,[3] some psychologist claim that words such as motives, need urges, wishes, and drives should not be used as synonyms; others are content to use them interchangeably.

The simple model shown in Figure 6.2.[4] indicated the relationship between needs, motives and objectives.

Fig.6.2 : Motivation Links, Needs and Objectives

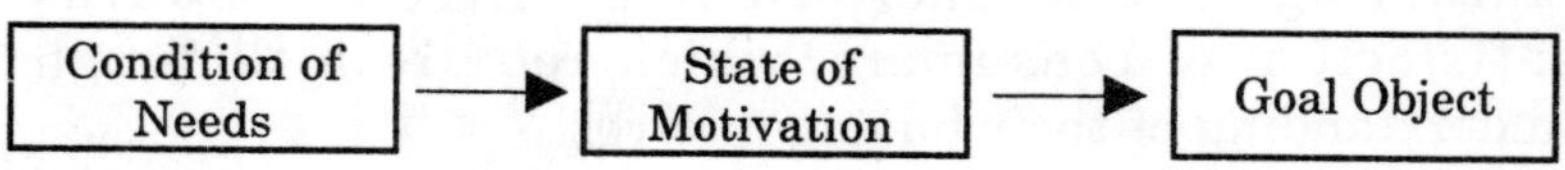

POSITIVE AND NEGATIVE MOTIVATION

According to psychologist, needs, wants, or desires are positive drives, and fear or aversions are negative drives.

The consumer is usually positive-drive-oriented when his choice for a particular product is based on purely objective criteria such as size, weight, price or miles per gallon. When some product is avoided in preference to some other product, subjective criteria, such as the desire for individuality, pride, fear, affection, and status operate. Usually drives based on objective criteria are emotional and negative.[5] Motives can come into conflict with each other, and thereby affecting consumer behaviour. The conflict would occur between two desirable alternatives (approach-approach conflict), or between two undesirable one (avoidance-avoidance conflict), or between a positive and a negative one (approach-approach conflict).[6]

Ballachey[7] distinguishes between positive driving forces which direct want towards objects, and negative forces which lead wants away from objects. Motives of fear may cause some people to avoid air travel unless alternative methods of transport are not available.

Customers-whether they are acting as personal customers or as buying agents for organizations-experience many kinds of need, an appreciation of the nature of needs would offer a valuable approach to the study of motivational influences on consumer behaviour.

EMERGENCE OF NEEDS AS FACTORS OF MOTIVATION

Any discussion of motivation is inevitably related to the study of needs. Between motives and needs exists interdependence: motives actuate and direct action to be taken in satisfaction of identified needs. Motivation acts an energizing force, which originates, sustains and directs activities towards diverse objectives. Through the stimuli of motives, men are inspired to achieve success in their professional and private lives; to acquire a host of desirable products; and to satisfy their needs for affiliation, prestige, power, and many of the other wants.

Successful marketing of goods and services of all kinds whether these relate to personal needs or to those of organization should be based on fundamental appreciation of motivation. How people will respond to marketing stimuli viz., price offers, advertising, product attributes, etc., is not always easy to predict. This leads the two American researcher[8] to comment: Human behaviour is so enormously varied, so delicately complex, so obscurely motivated that many people despair of findings valid generalizations to explain and predict the actions, thought, and feelings of human beings-despair, that is, of the very possibility of constructing a science of human behaviour. Perfect knowledge in any science is never attained, but this should discourage attempts to find out more about the wants of customers and the reasons why they buy their particular goods. Products are bought for the benefits, which it is anticipated they will give to the purchasers. Experienced marketers evaluate their products in terms of customer-expectations, and ensure that they build into their products valid reasons why people should buy from them, and not from their competitors. Obviously, this cannot be done successfully without sensitive awareness of the role of motives in buying behaviour.[9]

Needs have a knack of emerging one after another. According to motivational theorist, there exists a hierarchy of needs, and as lower needs are satisfied, higher needs arise. But success or failure in achieving a goal increases or decreases the intensity of the desire for fulfilling new needs. Consumer behaviour is considerably influenced or altered by post-achievements of goals. Continued deprivation of a primary goal, results in contentment with substitute goals. Failure to achieve a goal often leads to frustration, which further results in either aggression or withdrawal. Positive consumers usually resort to rationalization and substitute goals, which negatively-oriented consumers either withdraw or become aggressive.

MULTIPLICITY OF NEEDS

Two mangoes in one stone, they say in English but consumer behaviour in fact brings more. When a consumer sets a specific goal, in fact many needs are satisfied. Of the many motives that drive a consumer towards a particular product, the triggering motive serves as the prepotent. A single product may satisfy different needs and different products may satisfy the same need too. Bayton[10] cautiously remarks that an individual may be moved by not merely one need but more usually, a combination of needs. In this complex of needs, there is often one that is most dominant or prepotent. Human needs appear to be capable of almost infinite extension; as soon as one of the needs is satisfied, another appears in it place. This process is unending. It continues from birth to death.[11]

AROUSAL OF MOTIVES

Motives are aroused either by internal or external stimuli. Internal stimuli could be physiological or emotional and external stimuli cognitive or emotional or environmental. Motives have been classified as learned or unlearned, rational or emotional, conscious or unconscious, physical or psychological, etc., Emotional motives have been defined as those which have their origin in human instincts and emotions, giving rise to impulsive or non-rational responses. Copeland[12] believed that consumer goods were largely bought as a result of instinctive and emotional motivation.

MOTIVATIONAL RESEARCH

It is qualitative research trying to understand the working of the consumers' subconscious mind, perhaps the birth place of motives.[13] As motives are not things, they can not be measured objectively and accurately but with the help of psychology, motivational research tries to bring out the reasons of motives though it has not been as successful as claimed to be.

In order to develop an effective marketing strategy, marketers should analyse the geographic distribution and demographic composition of the population as a first step towards understanding the consumer characteristics, and that it must be analysed in segments. Significant shifts are occurring in regional population distribution patterns. Market differences traceable to differences in styles and ethnic backgrounds pose real challenge for marketing executives.

The regional distribution of population is important to marketing people because sectional difference lead to differences in the demand for many products. These differences can be traced to economic, social and other factors. Sociological patterns among consumers differ significantly. These patterns have considerable influence on buying behaviour. Per capita consumption of cosmetics and other beauty aids, for example, is much lower in one place and more in other places.

So an attempt is made here to find out the difference, if any, between the consumers, in terms of information sources used, factors of evaluating criteria, and the other selected variables. The behaviour of the consumers is studied to find out the differences among them. For this purpose, discriminant analysis is used to discriminate between the two populations.

FUNCTIONS OF DISCRIMINANT ANALYSIS

Discriminant functions is one of the most widely used multivariate procedures in behavioural research. It is a powerful tool, regarded as an univariate problem related to multiple regressions or a multivariate problem related to statistical tests. The process of discrimination that the statistical tool embodies is distinct from the process of classification that factor analysis embodies. The problem in discriminant analysis is finding a linear combination of variables that produce the maximum difference between the groups (usually two) considered for discrimination.

A simple linear discriminant function transforms an original set of measurements on a sample into a single discriminant score. That score, or transformed variable, represent the sample's position along a line defined by the linear discriminant function. Therefore, the discriminant function is a way of collapsing a multivariate problem down into a problem, which involves only one variable.

The test of significance may be derived form a 'distance' measure. This distance measure is the 'D^2' known as the 'Mahalanobis' distance (or the generalized distance). This distance is calculated from the two multivariate means and is expressed in units of the pooled variance. Further, the test may be transformed to an F-test. The null hypothesis tested by this statistics is that the two multivariate means are equal or that the distance between them is zero. The appropriateness of this as a test of discriminant function should be apparent. If the means of the two groups were very close together, it would be difficult to tell them apart, especially if both groups have large variance. In contrast, if the two means are well separated and the scatter about the means in small, discrimination will be relatively easy.[14]

However, there are two major ways in which discriminant function may be attempted. One is from the angle of the observations, so that each of the observations may be assigned discriminant score, which would help place it along the linear discriminant function line. This way, it would be possible to work towards the misclassification in the two sets of observation analysed. The alternative is to find the discriminant coefficients for the variables used in the discriminant function analysis. In this study, the former method is used to obtain discriminant scores for individuals (only selected interviewees) to speak specifically of consumer behaviour using these scores.

The Measures of Discriminant Function

The power of discriminant analysis lies in two of its properties for a measure-in fact, as index-of difference between the groups (two in this study) is one. In addition, it provides for an index on each of the observations in the two groups, which is the second. The power of this discriminant function therefore is to show the exact differences in the groups being discriminated against. Much more than that, it helps to allow each of the observations to be put on a discriminant function line, so that the position each holds with respect of the other may be known. This way, it becomes an effective tool of classification.

It would become a measure of difference between the groups of consumers and also help to classify the consumers into distinct groups, in as much as they differ in their behavioural characteristics. Some knowledge also can be gained on the 'misclassified' consumers, i.e., some of the consumers of public sector may show up the characteristics of the consumers of private sector and vice versa. These would form a class by themselves, in both the groups. Thus, the discrimination would be complete.

Groups for Discriminant Analyses

The study, as has been made clear in the earlier chapter pertains to consumer behaviour with respect to four products viz: Television, Refrigerator, Air-cooler and Washing machine- in the context of different types of areas: the consumers of public sector and private sector. The primary purpose behind the selection of areas-begin that behaviour would be quite different because of the milieu differences. In discriminating the two groups of samples, three groups of variables have been taken; the first group of variables is the same as that used in the factor analysis (15 variables in all); the second group of variables consists of (3 variables) relating to information sources (personal, commercial and retail outlet, and hence so designated), and the third group consists of such variables and number of shops visited before purchases (4 variables in all). The products, four of them as indicated, are discriminated against with three groups of variables for the study areas. In effect the sample consumers of study areas are discriminated against each other's, using the three sets of variables.

The results of the analyses are such that each of the three groups of variables has a mean, standard deviation, discriminant coefficient, and the difference are deduced form differences in the three measures. Also, the group differences are measured by 'D^2' and tested for significance by F test value.

Discriminant coefficients have been worked out for observations for the groups being discriminated against each other. So much so, it has been tried to get only a glimpse of how people think while in purchase of a product. Now an attempt is made to discriminating the people through the discriminant analysis. Generating discriminant scores for the individual observations has done it. But in doing so, liberty has been taken to take random selections from the sample.

The computer runs were made individually for the four products (television, refrigerator, air-cooler and washing machine) using the three sets of variables as indicated earlier: 15 variables, 4 variables such as brands available are considered, mode of payment and shops visited prior to purchase, and 3 variables exclusively of sources of information. In all, twelve runs were made and the results are summarized.

The results derived of discriminant analyses for consumers from the different samples for the four products have given surprisingly very small differences in all cases: this is contrary to the perception of differing milieus. However, in all cases, the null hypothesis that there is no difference between the groups discriminated against for the 'Mahalanobis' distance function gives the following results.

Table 6.1 : Mahalanobis Distance Function

For 15 variables case	Television	0.002372
	Refrigerator	0.001897
	Air-Cooler	0.001513
	Washing Machine	0.001674
For 4 variables case	Televisio	0.000496
	Refrigerator	0.000240
	Air-Cooler	0.000235
	Washing Machine	0.000210
For 3 variables case	Television	0.000139
	Refrigerator	0.000128
	Air-Cooler	0.000069
	Washing Machine	0.000116

(**Source :** Primary Data).

These distance values, although very small, do indicate differences among the samples from the study areas. In sum, there is a difference, distinctly perceptible, between the two groups compared. It indicated the relative position of each of the individual consumers through the discriminant scores. It should be noticed that nearly all distribution is about the group means, referred to as 'R1' for group 1 public sector and 'R2' for group 2 private sectors. As expected, the consumers cluster around the means.[15]

It is at once apparent that there are several misclassifications. This means that some consumers who belong to public sector in fact belong to private sector and vice versa. This means that some people despite living in one kind of milieu express in effect another kind of milieu. A majority of the consumers cluster around the means, which is as should be in a normal distribution. However, nearly a third are beyond the central cluster, representing the large differences in their purchase behaviour. In an ideal situation, the central cluster should contain most of the observations, while in a real case, a good number of observations always fall outside of the central cluster.

FACTORS INFLUENCING IN DECISION- MAKING

The percent of contribution each variable makes to the overall influence in the 15 variables, 4 variables and 3 variables cases are given in the accompanying tables. It would appear that the good determinant factor influencing the consumer behaviour with respect to each of the products concerned differ radically, and the contribution to discrimination is also very wide, form one to the other. Taking 15 variables case for the four products, it could be said that there are variables that make both

positive and negative contributions to discrimination, and that negative contribution is offset in most cases by larger contribution (in per cent terms) by others. (Contributions when added give 100 per cent. This addition needs to be product-wise).

15 Variables Case

Television

The determinant factors influencing the consumer behaviour for television are summarized in Table 6.2. From the Table, it could be noticed that out of fifteen variables, which are selected as the basis for discrimination, warranty contributes more which accounts for 27.31 per cent and it also could be considered as a good determinant factor influencing the consumer behaviour in the purchase of television. Since the cash involvement is more in the case of television purchases, it is no doubt that warranty is a good determinant factor. Because of many possible breakdowns that usually occur in electronic goods, the consumer pays attention to warranty period, so that he can reduce / avoid the service costs.

Table 6.2 : Determinant Factors Influencing the Consumer Behaviour for Television (15 Variables case)

Sl. No.	*Variables*	*Percent of Contribution*	*Rank in Order*
1.	Warranty	27.31	1
2.	Dealer location	19.83	2
3.	Dealer reputation	12.13	3
4.	Special gift	12.00	4
5.	Easy installments	7.68	5
6.	Appearance, style, colour	5.93	6
7.	Lower price	4.61	7
8.	Special discount	2.52	8
9.	Equal price	2.43	9
10.	Immediate availability	0.46	10
11.	Price contest	0.03	11
12.	Technical features	-0.02	12
13.	Availability of spares/ services	-0.09	13
14.	Brand popularity	-0.40	14
15.	Ease of operation	-0.57	15

(**Source :** Primary Data).

Dealer location comes next (19.83) for the discrimination between the populations. Location of the dealers, since it involves transportation charges, definitely must be another determinant factor influencing the behaviour of the consumer.

Dealer reputation and special gift contributes equally (12 per cent) for discrimination between the population: So dealer reputation could be considered as a good determinant factor, influencing the consumer behaviour in the television purchases. This could be for the simple reason that the reputed dealers can give dependable after-sales service and in time than the small dealers. Even if the manufacturer's service network fails, they may have their own service network to attend immediately, which the small dealers cannot afford. In addition to this, they can offer some other facilities like free installation, door delivery, attractive cash discounts etc.

Special gift, which is offered at times by the dealers, may attract the consumers and that could be the reason that it acts as a good determinant factors of influence on consumer behaviour in the purchase of television.

Easy installment as a variable contributes 7.68 per cent for discrimination, and other variables are contributing either with low/negative percent, which need not be discussed here.

Refrigerator

The percentages of contribution for discrimination for refrigerator purchasers are given in Table 6.3. Special gift as a variable contributes 93.64 per cent heavily for discrimination, since every consumer will be waiting for the offer given by the dealers. So it could be considered as a very good determinant factor influencing the consumer behaviour of refrigerator buyers.

It could be noticed form the Table that appearance, style, design etc., contributes 29.89 per cent for discriminating between the populations. Appearance and design matters much, as the need and purpose differ among consumers. Size also matters much according to the number of members in the family.

Table 6.3 : Determinant Factors Influencing the Consumer Behaviour for Refrigerator (15 Variables Case)

Sl. No.	*Variables*	*Percent of Contribution*	*Rank in Order*
1.	Special gift	93.64	1
2.	Appearance, style, colour	29.89	2
3.	Dealer reputation	27.82	3
4.	Ease of operation	25.75	4
5.	Dealer location	21.53	5
6.	Brand popularity	6.17	6
7.	Price contest	5.45	7
8.	Easy installments	1.72	8
9.	Immediate availability	-2.14	9
10.	Warranty	-2.18	10
11.	Equal price	-3.12	11
12.	Availability of spares/ services	-3.46	12
13.	Special discount	-11.01	13
14.	Lower price	-23.91	14
15.	Technical features	-71.73	15

(**Sources:** Primary Data).

Dealer reputation and ease of operation contributes 27.82 percent and 25.75 per cent respectively towards discrimination. The reason definitely must be the same as discussed in the previous pages. Dealer location contributes 21.53 per cent for discrimination, as too technical operation may not be easy for all the members in the family. Other variables contribute lesser and even negatively, and hence need not be discussed.

Air-cooler

The determinant factor influencing the consumer in percent-wise for air-cooler buyers are given in Table 6.4. It is very interesting to note that 'Equal Price' as a variable contributes 119.82 per cent towards discrimination, stressing that it is a very good determinant factor influencing the consumer behaviour of air-cooler buyers. Once the consumer decided to go in for any product, it is the human tendency that they have to get it immediately. Particularly, air-cooler, an important machine which is used in the household during summer season, housewife may not be willing to postpone the purchase. The price of all the brands of air-cooler in India is almost equal, and hence it could be considered as good determinant factor influencing the consumer behaviour. So equal price of the product could be considered as a good determinant factor influencing the consumer behaviour of air-cooler purchasers.

Table 6.4 : Determinant Factors Influencing the Consumer Behaviour for Air-Cooler (15 Variables Case)

Sl. No.	*Variables*	*Percent of Contribution*	*Rank in Order*
1.	Equal price	119.82	1
2.	Immediate availability	54.13	2
3.	Special gift	49.36	3
4.	Brand popularity	18.38	4
5.	Dealer location	13.61	5
6.	Special discount	5.47	6
7.	Price contest	4.16	7
8.	Dealer reputation	-0.81	8
9.	Easy installments	-2.15	9
10.	Warranty	-7.57	10
11.	Lower price	-16.01	11
12.	Appearance, style, colour	-16.79	12
13.	Ease of operation	-20.48	13
14.	Technical features	-33.82	14
15.	Availability of spares/ Services	-70.12	15

(**Sources:** Primary Data).

Immediate availability contributes 54.13 per cent towards discrimination. In India, some leading and popular brands may not be available immediately. Special gift here also contributes 49.36 per cent towards discrimination, and it could be for the same reason discussed above.

Brand popularity contributes 18.38, which could be considered as good determinant factor influencing the consumer behaviour. The reason is in most of the markets for each product a number of brands are available. There is no product for which alternative brand is not available; some of them are more popular than others for various factors. The popularity is generally decided by market share of a particular brand, the data for which is regularly published in newspaper and magazines. The consumers of air-cooler give due weightage to the aspect and feel that a product that has higher market share than others is rated high in choice making by a consumer.

Dealer location contributes 13.61 per cent, which could be for the simple reason that the product may require regular service and hence the closeness of the dealer is required. Other variables contribute lesser and negatively and hence are not explained here.

Washing Machine

The determinant factor influencing the consumer for washing machine buyers are presented in Table 6.5. Easy installment contributes 53.73 per cent towards discrimination. As most of the middle- class consumers cannot afford cash purchases, the only way out is installment. So it could be considered as a good determinant factor influencing the consumer behaviour of washing machine buyers.

From the Table, it could be noticed that warranty and dealer reputation contributes highly towards discrimination, and hence they could be considered as good determinant factor, influencing the consumer behaviour of washing machine buyers. Warranty accounts for 45.81 per cent and dealer reputation accounts for 41.71 per cent.

Availability of spares and service contributes 41.35 per cent, and equal price accounts for 31.54 per cent towards

Table 6.5 : Determinant Factors Influencing the Consumer Behaviour for Washing Machine (15 Variables Case)

Sl. No.	*Variables*	*Percent of Contribution*	*Rank in Order*
1.	Easy installments	53.73	1
2.	Warranty	45.81	2
3.	Dealer reputation	41.71	3
4.	Availability of spares/ services	41.35	4
5.	Equal price	31.54	5
6.	Dealer location	21.54	6
7.	Ease of operation	17.18	7
8.	Special gift	11.49	8
9.	Price contest	-2.97	9
10.	Appearance, style, colour	-8.16	10
11.	Immediate availability	-9.56	11
12.	Special discount	-17.23	12
13.	Brand popularity	-20.07	13
14.	Technical features	-45.61	14
15.	Lower price	-56.28	15

(**Source** : Primary Data).

discrimination. Dealer location also matters much for the washing machine as it contributes 21.54 per cent for discrimination. Other variables contribute lesser and negatively and are not discussed here.

Variables Case

In analyzing the determinant factor, influencing the consumer behaviour, three variables were chosen as sources of information, namely, personal, commercial, and retail outlet sources.

From Table 6.6, commercial sources are the overwhelmingly good determinant factor, influencing the consumer behaviour in the case of refrigerator (217.43 per cent) and air-cooler (204.17 per cent). In the case of television, commercial sources are very important, even more than personal and retail outlets. The retail outlet sources become secondarily important in the case of air-cooler. As for washing machine, however only personal sources are very important and retail outlet only secondarily. As for air-cooler, personal sources are not important at all, for they determine highly negatively.

Table 6.6 : Determinant Factors Influencing the Consumer Behaviour for All four Durable products (3 Variables Case)

		Per cent of Contribution			
Sl. No.	*Variables*	*Television*	*Refri-gerator*	*Air-cooler*	*Washing machine*
1.	Personal sources	5.69	-57.67	-244.53	81.91
2.	Commercial sources	60.12	217.43	204.17	-5.05
3.	Retail outlet sources	34.19	-59.76	140.36	23.14
	Total	100.00	100.00	100.00	100.00

(**Sources:** Primary Data).

In sum, commercial sources are good determinant factor influencing the consumer behaviour in the cases of television, refrigerator and air-cooler; personal sources in the case of washing machine only, and retail outlets in the case of air-cooler, television and washing machine in sequential.

4 VARIABLES CASE

The other factors that could be considered are (i) number of shops visited before purchase, (ii) number of brands considered, (iii) mode of payment and (iv) number of brands available (at the time of purchase). Each of these factors may have in some way determined and influenced consumer behaviour is a reasonable assumption, and hence to be verified here.

The determinant factor, influencing the consumer behaviour for 4 variables case is summarized in Table 6.7. The variables 'number of shops visited' and 'number of brands available' as can be seen from the table have contributed negatively to purchase in most cases, although only in the case of television, the number of brands available at the time of purchase in the market contributed marginally to the behaviour pattern discernible. Mode of payment, most importantly installments, has contributed generously to the behaviour is borne out by the fact of contribution available from the discriminant analysis.

Table 6.7 : Determinant Factors Influencing the Consumer Behaviour for all Four Durable Products (4 Variables Case)

Sl. No.	Variables	*Per cent of Contribution*			
		Television	*Refri-gerator*	*Air-cooler*	*Washing machine*
1.	No. of shops visited	-2.45	-290.12	-51.49	-36.71
2.	No. of brands considered	38.63	478.72	-29.74	-3.63
3.	Mode of payment	35.57	51.63	271.63	147.69
4.	No. of brands available	28.25	-140.23	-90.4	-7.35
	Total	100.00	100.00	100.00	100.00

(**Sources:** Primary Data).

For instance, in the case of air cooler, the mode of payment alone is the good determinant factor, influencing the consumer behaviour, and all the other three variables have contributed only negatively, and hence the larger percent of 271.63. It has contributed also generously to the purchase of washing machine, while only less so in the case of refrigerator and television. It must be remembered that the latter two products are relatively highly priced than that of air-cooler and washing machine, and there usually is reluctancy on the part of the consumers to go for a considerable amount from the monthly budgets of the families to which the respondents belonged. Hence, it is understandable as a good determinant factor influencing the behaviour in the case of air cooler and washing machine (which involve small installments over a short duration) and less so in the case of refrigerator and television. It is only in the case of refrigerator and less so in the case of television that the number of brands considered had any say and hence consumer behaviour.

SECTION SUMMARY

The main findings of this chapter could be summarized as follows.

The Distance Measure or 'Mahalonobis' Function shows that there are appreciable differences between the consumers, although the distance is too small in many cases. The distance is comparatively more, particularly in relation to 15 variables cases i.e., variables of evaluative criteria.

After finding out that the difference exists between the populations, the variable, which contributes more for discrimination, are examined.

Determinant Factors Influencing the Consumer Behaviour

In the case of 15 variables case, it could be seen that dealer reputation (rather the easy accessibility), warranty and special gift are very important for the consumers in all products. That is why they have been rated as good determinant factor, influencing the consumer behaviour in all the four products. It could be noticed that no variable is consistently a good determinant factor, influencing the consumer behaviour for all the four durable products.

In 3 variables case, it could be summed up that commercial sources are a good determinant factor, influencing the consumer behaviour in television, refrigerator, and air-cooler, while personal source is a good determinant factor, influencing the consumer behaviour for washing machine buyers.

In 4 variables case, the number of brands considered acts as a good determinant factor, influencing the consumer behaviour in television and refrigerator, while mode of payment acts as a good determinant factor, influencing the consumer behaviour almost in all the four durable products, but heavily in air-cooler and washing machine, and it is the only variable, which positively contributes in all the four durable products.

REFERENCES AND NOTES

1. Leon G. Schiffman, and Leslie Lazar Kanuk, (1990), "Consumer Behaviour", Prentice-Hall of India Private Limited, (3rd ed.), New Delhi, p.67.
2. Ibid. p. 68.
3. James A.Bayton, (1958), "Motivation, Cognition, Learning-Basic Factors in Consumer Behaviour", *Journal of Marketing,* January, 22,Vol. VII, p.25.
4. Peter M, Chisnall, (1975), "Marketing-A Behavioural Analysis", and London: McGraw-Hill, p. 39.
5. Peters Winberg, and Wolfgang Gottwald, (1982), "Impulsive Consumer Buying as a Result of Emotions", *Journal of Business Research,* Vol. 10, pp. 43-57.
6. Abraham H. Maslow, (1943), "A Theory of Human Motivation Psychological Review", Vol.50, pp. 370-396.
7. David Krech, Richard S.Crutchfield, and Egerton L. Bellachey, (1962), "Individual in Society", McGraw-Hill, New York, p.52.
8. Bernard Berelson and Gary A. Steiner, (1964), "Human Behaviour: An Inventory of Scientific Finding", Harcourt, Brace and World, New York, p. 97.
9. Peter M. Cisnall, Op.cit. p. 39.
10. Bayton, Op.cit. p. 30.
11. M.T. Copeland, (1924), "Principles of Merchandising Chicago": A.W. Shaw, New York, p. 62.
12. Goleman, Daniel, (1984), "New View of Minds Gives Unconscious and Expanded Role", New York Times, February 7, p.5.
13. W.T. Trucker, (1964), "The Development of Brand Loyalty", *Journal of Marketing Research,* August, Vol. 12, p. 33.
14. W. Cooley and P. Lohnes, (1962), "Multivariate Procedures for the Behavioural Sciences", New York: Wiley, pp. 119-123.
15. M. Tatsuoka, (1970), "Discriminant Analysis: The Study of Group Differences", Champaign, III: Institute for Personality and Ability Testing, New York, p. 65.

7

Summary and Conclusion

PROBLEM FOCUS

The present report has hitherto discussed in detail the results of the study on certain aspects of purchase decisions and consumer behaviour with respect to select durable items in the urban areas of Vellore District.

As all the consumers are not alike and their preferences are constantly changing; they prefer differentiated products, which reflect their own special needs, personalities, and lifestyles. People prefer a specific model of durable products among different competing brands for various reasons like handling, comfort, price, appearance, and durability.

Consumers are highly involved in a purchase when it is expensive, bought infrequently and risky. Products involve a decision-making unit, which consists of more than a single person. In a competing market, an analysis of factors that influence purchase decisions is a pre-requisite for the decision-makers of a planned economy because it enables them to have an understanding of the current and future demands of durable products, and match supply with the changing pattern of demand, which will have a great competitive advantage in the market place.

After the World War II, the sellers' market has disappeared and buyers' market has come up. Thus, the marketers of durable products, who understand the relative importance of the information sources used by the consumers, the differences between the users and non-users of the particular sources of information, with reference to selected variables, the evaluation criteria used in making the final decision, and the factors influencing the consumers decision-making process, have a great competitive advantage in the market place. So far, no serious attempts have been made in this field of study in India. The present study of "Purchase decision and consumer behaviour of users of durable products" is an attempt in that direction.

The consumer may perceive product information from several sources. The source, which exposes the product and its features and/or the source, which helps the consumer in making the final choice, is of great importance to marketers to decide on their selling and advertising strategies. However, in the very competitive marketing situation prevailing, the manufacturers or the product dealers do want to understand the consumers' decision-making behaviour in the purchase of the products they manufacture and sell. The factors determining decisions are important for them in so far as they help them make some managerial decisions. The diversity of the Indian consumer milieus poses serious challenge to marketing communications. It is because the psychographical profiles of the Indian consumers vary widely, from one segment to another, and sometimes within the milieu.

Therefore, the approach to a study of perceptions and purchase behaviour is somewhat complex in orientation. The study concerns itself with two sets of variables: that of information sources, and that which are considered the evaluative criteria. The sources of information are grouped into three broad categories: (a) personal sources, (b) commercial sources, and (c) retail outlet sources. The evaluative criteria and price (equal and cheaper), model qualities such as appearance, colour and style, brand popularity, availability of services, and spares, product performance, installments payment, availability of the products, ease of operation, reputation and locational attributes of dealers, discounts, and warranty. Besides these, some other variables have also been considered as they have impacts on purchase decisions.

The study sets the following objectives for analysis. (i) to examine the relative importance of the information sources used by the consumers in the purchase of four consumer durable products. (ii) to find out the differences between the users and non-users of the particular sources of information in the search process and the dependency of certain selected variables,(iii) to analyse the evaluation criteria used in making the final decision,(iv) to identify the factors influencing the consumers in the decision-making process.

THE DIMENSIONS

A brief sketch of the Vellore district serves as the backdrop of the study on the purchase decisions and consumer behaviour with respect to select durable items. The physical features of the district, size of population and their occupation, the trend in urbanization, administrative divisions, land use pattern, size of holdings, irrigations, cropping pattern, industrial development – large scale industries, small scale industries khadi and village industries, employment in public and private sector, Trade and commerce, development of infrastructures like roads, motor vehicles on road, railways, electricity and its consumption, housing development, financial institutions, particularly commercial banks, distribution of loans, small saving collection, health and standard of living of the people do exert influence on the purchase decisions of the consumers in this region.

The hot climate, prevailing in Vellore district, induces the middle and upper class people to purchase refrigerator and air coolers. The employment and high income have motivated the people to purchase television sets and washing machine. The population, size of family and the nature of occupation would determine the size of income of the families. Agriculture is the primary occupation of the majority of people in the district. The development of agriculture depends on the land use pattern, size of holdings, crop pattern and irrigation.

The rapid urbanization is the result of growing industrialization of the Vellore district. The large and small-scale industries, khadi and village industries, leather industries, trade and commerce have contributed to the development of industries and employment.

The developments of infrastructures like roads, transports, railways, electricity and housing have changed the industrial face of the Vellore district. The people's preference for modern living, which is augmented by the consumption loans, distributed by the commercial banks, has led to the purchase and possession of more and more durable commodities. The contribution to small savings, healthy living, and better standard of living have motivated the people to develop a positive outlook towards durable assets.

THE APPROACH

The following concepts, used in the study, are reviewed:

- Evaluation of Consumer Information in Economic Thought.
- The Role of Information in Marketing.
- The Behaviour Models.
- Market Information.
- Risk and the Bayesian Approach.
- Nature of Information Sources.
- Market Originating Information.
- Consumer Oriented Information.
- Information Search.
- Evaluation Criteria.
- Evaluation Criteria Process.
- Decision Making Process.

- Factors Influencing the Consumer Behaviour in Decision Making.
- Operational Definitions.

The research design, chosen for the present study, includes the choice of the study area, the selection of sample, collection of data and the tools used for analysis.

The Vellore district has been purposively selected for the present study as it has large number of towns, with concentration of large and small-scale industries. Out of the nine Municipal towns, four towns viz., Vellore, Gudiyattam, Vanyambadi, and Tirupattur towns were chosen as they have largest number of dealer shops for the selected durable goods.

The consumers of the selected durable goods were traced through the dealers of durable goods in the selected towns. There were thirty dealers, distributed in the four towns, dealing in durable goods- television, refrigerator, air cooler, and washing machine. From the selected dealers, 20 consumers, who purchased the above said items, were identified. There were 600 consumers of durable goods in the sample frame. Pre-tested questionnaires were served to the selected consumers. Only 450 filled up questionnaires were returned to the researcher through the dealers.

A structured questionnaire was used to collect the required details from the consumers. The questionnaire was suitably amended after the pre-test through a pilot study. It comprises two sections: Section 'A' was framed to obtain details about the information sources, and section 'B' to collect general information about the consumers of four durable products.

The secondary sources of data on physical features, population, land utilization, agricultural development, industrial development, infra structure development, health and standard of living were collected from published sources and from the Statistical Department of the Vellore district and the state.

The collected data were analysed with the help of simple averages, percentages and pie-diagrams. Chi-Square was used as a test of independent.

The samples have been used with reference to data gathered in generating factor structures for the products in order to break the variables down to a smaller number of factors that explain the dimensions of consumer perceptions and also decisions.

The same data have been subjected to a further analysis of discrimination so as to bring out the differences between the population with respect to factor, influencing the consumer in making purchase decision and perception variables, sources of information and other related variables that determine consumer behaviour in some way. In the two analyses, the study has attempted to gain insights into the consumer behaviour of the two groups of consumers (public sector and private sector) as well as classify the respondents into definable groups showing particular characteristics.

The two analyses tested some theoretical suppositions and tried to provide for a classification of variables and consumers, and at the same time, explicitly explaining their behaviours and decisions. Additionally, the study has also looked into information use, the role of media in their perceptions about the durables and how they have helped making decisions for final purchases.

The examination of information sources has been made with a view to find out (a) exposure and (b) effectiveness, in as much as the consumers' first hand knowledge of products and brands and further, in using this knowledge gained, in making a purchase decision. In fact, the processes of acquisition through media exposure and the actual purchase have been conceived as two distinct stages of consumer behaviour in which the consumers go through a period of evaluation and decision. In as much as these two stages become effective, the relative importance of exposure and effectiveness has been fully evaluated. The evaluation of these two (exposure and effectiveness) was taken to its logical analysis of the dependency between information sources vis-à-vis other selected variables, such as the number of shops/ showrooms visited, number of brands considered before the purchase decision was made with respect to the four products. The time lags between contemplation and actual purchase have also been considered to bring out insights on the planning part of a purchase.

In each case, again, the number of factors extracted depended very much on the data and the power of the technique. The rule, applied in respect of extraction of factors, is that the 'eigen values' should in each factor be more than 1.0, and this was followed for the express purpose of making interpretation worthwhile.

The discriminant analysis was performed with two particular views in mind, and the first was to see how different were the consumers in terms of their milieus, what and how many groups would they form in any given discrimination and identify the factor influencing the consumer in making purchase decision. The testing, however, was to see whether the samples, or at least most of them, fall in line with normal distribution. The results have been rewarding and salutary in that the applications have accomplished the classifications of variables into "factors" and people into "groups". The results have thrown sufficient light on the perceptions and behaviour of the consumers. The variety that the results indicate is something that gains us a look into the minds of people making decisions.

THE RESULTS

Information Sources Used by the Consumers

Most of the consumers have shown commercial source as the most important in terms of both exposure value and effectiveness criterion. This shows indirectly of the relatively higher exposure to commercial information in study areas, expresses the access to commercial sources and the influence it has on purchase decisions. The consumers place more of a premium on commercial information, as there is less of time for personal contacts.

But, in the study areas, there is some time lag in decision making after having been exposed to sources of information. While this time lag indicates a period of evaluation on the one hand, this also makes clear the relative importance of the sources themselves. Personal sources make for quick decisions, while commercials cause a slightly delayed decision, perhaps, because some form of verification goes into the making of it. But the personal and the commercial sources influence all the consumers. The users of personal sources took time, one to four weeks, while the users of commercial sources took more than four weeks.

Users and Non-Users of Information Sources

When users and non-users of sources of information were pitted against each other, they did show significant differences in time taken for decisions. This is particularly so in the case of users of commercial and retail outlet sources. Time taken is independent to personal source, while it is dependent for the other two sources in the sample areas.

The two groups of consumers, however, relate same views on planning the purchase in which all the three information sources have been evaluated and acted upon. Both users and non-users do not show differences in terms of the sources in the sample. The level of planning is dependent on all the three sources for all consumers.

The number of brands, considered in purchase decisions, is dependent, relative to all the sources for all the consumers, while independent relative to commercial and retail outlet sources. In final purchase, conversely, the users of these sources consider one or two brands only, which incidentally, is a result of brand popularity and availability.

The number of shops visited before a purchase decision is one or two for all the consumers. The percentage is rather equal in relation to the users of retail outlet source among the total population where they have visited more than two shops.

Evaluative Criteria in Purchase Decisions

The factor analytical procedure was applied for the four products using 15 variables. The most important factor structures bring out the following evaluation criteria used by the respondents.

Respondents	*Television*	*Refrigerator*	*Air-cooler*	*Washing Machine*
Factor-1	Installment and price	After-sales service and prize	Ease of operation and prize	Warranty and dealer attributes
Factor-2	Price, Model and discount	Price	Dealer attributes and ease of operation	Discount and dealer attributes

Considering only the first two dimensions for each product in the samples, the finding for television is that the main dimension is installment and price for all the consumers. While price is the common composite variable for the samples, installment appears to be more important for the sample. The reason is that either there are several hire-purchase offers in urban areas, or installment buying is taking advantage of such offers. In terms of the bipolar, there is near conformity for price and model quality in the samples, although discount is an incentive for urban buyers.

Refrigerator appears to generate disparate factors in both the main and the bipolar. After-sales service and prize are the first dimensions in the sample, primarily because after-sales services are a must and prize is the usual or at least the single mode by which such expensive items are got. Price is the common link in the bipolar for the samples.

Air-cooler, the first dimension for all the consumers, is a composite of ease of operation and prize. Prize is therefore the common link. Ease of operation is important for all the consumers mainly for quick work. Ease of operation gets tagged with dealer attributes for all the consumers. There is some reinforcing on ease of operation for all the consumers because it appears once again in the bipolar.

As for washing machine, however, the factor analysis procedure was employed for the aggregate of the total samples, considering that they were long introduced to the product, and they do not in fact show much difference in preferences, uses and purchase decisions. Warranty and dealer attributes form the first dimension and discount and dealer attributes, the bipolar. The inclusion of dealer attributes in all the dimensions is important as it reinforces the value of the same when all the samples get aggregated together. However, warranty is the single most important dimension for all the consumers.

In all products, the consumers seem to put a premium on price while they may differ explicitly on the availability, dealer location and reputation, technical performance, discount and the like. The consumers prefer as most important a set of variables, whatever may be the set, but there are some common ones, and some disparate variables. Yet among the products, the results of analysis provide for some perspective: for instance, in all these products, the evaluative criteria appears to be economic or utility aspect rather than psychological.

Determinant Factor Influencing the Consumer in Making Purchase Decision

The discrimination, when effected with varying number of variables, gives rise to incisive insights into the differences between the two groups of consumers (private sector and public sector). Two viewpoints emerge from discriminant analyses of the public sector and private sector samples. Firstly, there are slight differences between the consumers from the two areas as may be understood from the Mahalonobis distance criterion as well as in terms of the F-test for significance. Secondly, a majority in both cluster around the means, meaning the samples are drawn from normally distributed populations. However, the number of groups indicates that there are extremes in both samples and the milieu swapping (where one group exemplifies the milieu of the other, while at the same time belonging to the other) is common.

The factors influencing the consumer behaviour according to rank are given as under:

15 Variables Case (First three ranks only)

Rank	*Television*	*Refrigerator*	*Air-Cooler*	*Washing Machine*
1.	Warranty	Special gift	Equal price	Easy installments
2.	Dealer location	Appearance, colour, style etc.	Immediate availability	Warranty
3.	Dealer reputation	Dealer reputation	Special gift	Dealer reputation

3 Variables Case (First rank only)

Rank	*Television*	*Refrigerator*	*Air-Cooler*	*Washing Machine*
1.	Commercial	Commercial	Commercial	Personal

4 Variables Case (First rank only)

Rank	*Television*	*Refrigerator*	*Air-Cooler*	*Washing Machine*
1.	No. of brands considered	No. of brands Considered	Mode of Payment	Mode of Payment

The analysis, using 15 variables (those used to identify the evaluation criteria), provides for determinant factor influencing the consumer behaviour for the purchase of the durable products. For television, warranty, dealer location and dealer reputation are the three most important contributors. For refrigerator, special gift, appearance, style and colour (model qualities) as a means of acquisition, and dealer reputation are the three most important contributors. For air-cooler, on the other hand, equal price, immediate availability, and special gift, are the three most important contributors. For washing machine, easy installments, warranty and dealer reputation, are the three most important contributors. Thus, the varied nature of contributors becomes apparent. Yet, dealer attributes at least appear to be a high contributor in terms of percent added to discrimination.

Using the three sources of information as variables to discriminate the samples, the linear function yields the following. Commercial source is the largest contributor to discrimination in purchase decisions of three products, viz., television, refrigerator and air-cooler, while personal source is the largest contributor for the other product, viz., washing machine.

Using four other related variables in discrimination of the samples, the number of brands considered emerges as the largest contributor in television and refrigerator while mode of payment in air-cooler and washing machines. However, in all products, mode of payment contributes consistently positive, and that is the only variable with positive contribution to the discrimination in all the products.

CONCLUSION

Information Sources

The information sources, which are used by the consumer, are divided into three sections namely (1) personal sources (2) commercial sources (including mass media) and (3) retail outlet sources. Personal sources include information from friends, relatives, and neighbors, past experience with the product, personal observation and examination. Commercial source includes advertisement in newspapers, magazines, books, pamphlets, consumer reports, radio, television, roadside hoardings and movie [cinema]. Retail outlet source includes information from salesmen, personal shop visits and retail outlet. Hence, it is observed that the above three sources of information are mostly used by the consumers in taking decision in the purchase of durable products.

The variables taken as evaluative criteria for purchase decisions are price [equal and cheaper], brand popularity, availability of the product, reputation and location of the dealer, technical performance, service and availability of spare-parts, model qualities [size, colour, style etc.], warranty, discounts and gifts.

An analysis of evaluation criteria shows that the consumers opt for a good product.

Information Sources and Pre-purchase Behaviour

The following inferences are derived from discourse and discussion.

The commercial source has formed as an important item of exposure and effectiveness to the sample consumers.

The consumers utilized the personal sources and retail outlet sources for one to four weeks in decision-making, while the commercial sources they used more than four weeks. While scrutinizing the relationship between time and information sources, the former personal sources found to be independent, and the latter commercial and retail outlet sources proved to be a dependent factor.

The consumers have carefully planned before every purchase. So, the level of planning is considered to be a dependent factor related to all other information sources.

Most of the sample consumers have visited one or two shops or show rooms in making purchase decision, but more than two or more shops in case of retail outlet sources. The variables are dependent on each other in the samples.

Inspite of so many information sources, the consumers are drawn towards one or two brands at their final decision, but still brands are proved to be a dependent factor in relation to the three information sources.

Demographic and socio-economic characteristics are deemed to be independent variables with few exceptions like their age, sex and personal view derived from information sources.

Evaluation Criteria in Purchase Decision

Out of fifteen variables, only first two factors ie., main dimension and bipolar are necessary for the purpose of our epitome and conclusion.

Among the evaluation criteria used in purchase decision the most striking factor is "price", which stands first compared to other variables like installment, discount, prize and gift scheme. Consumers give more importance to economic development or utility in the price of television, refrigerator and air cooler.

With regard to the fourth product, washing machine, price and easy installment are the important criteria used.

The consumers also expressed their preference for goods with discount, easy installment, reputation, operational ease and service charges.

Operational ease also weighed heavily with air-cooler product rather than television, refrigerator and washing machine.

Determinant Factors Influencing the Consumer Behaviour

In fifteen variables case, the dealer reputation, warranty and special gift are judged to be important factors by the consumers in the purchase of all the four durable products.

In three variables case, the dealers have been rated as good determinant factor in influencing the behaviour of the consumers to buy television, refrigerator and air – cooler. But personal source is considered to be a good determinant factor influencing the consumer especially for washing machine.

In four variables case, the brand occupies a good determinant and lead to positive aspect in influencing the consumers to buy more Televisions and Refrigerators. Mode of payment also acts as a good determinant factor, influencing the consumer behaviour in the purchase of air cooler and washing machine.

SUGGESTIONS FOR FURTHER RESEARCH

Based on the present study, it is felt that two major fields of research emerge for consideration of further research.

Firstly, an attempt could be made to consider the personality factors of the consumers and their relevance to the evaluative criteria. In other words, are there certain personality characteristics that influence the choice process?.

Secondly, instead of finding out what evaluative criteria made a person to buy particular product, it must be worth knowing as to what made him buy that product at all when there are many other needs that are to be met. This process must help to understand how one sets his priority in using his income?.

Finally, choice in the purchase of products and the buyers' perceived value of such choices may even be looked into, in as much as choice process in the decision-making can be. Again, consumer behaviour may be studied in the context of diffusion studies wherein one could look into information sources and their impacts on consumer behaviour as well as simulating such behaviour.

Bibliography

BOOKS

Adler & Crespi I., (1968), "Attitude Research on The Rocks", American Marketing Association, Chicago.

Amarchand D. & Varadarajan B., (1994), "An Introduction to Marketing", 1st edition, Vikas Publishing House Private Limited. Kent Publishing Co., New Delhi, 2nd ed.

Assael, Henry, (1983), "Consumer Behaviour and Marketing Action," Boston:

Barkley, Bruce T. and James H. Saylor, (1994), "Customer-Driven Project Management : A New Paradigm in Total Quality Implementation", McGraw-Hill,. New York.

Basumhart, Raymond C., (1968), "Ethics in Business", Holt, Rinehart and Winston Inc.,. New York.

Batra, Promod, (1994), "Simple Ways to Make Your Customers Happy", Think Inc., New Delhi.

Bernard Berelson and Gary A. Steinev, (1964), "Human Behaviour", Harcourt, Brace and World,. New York.

Bennett, Peter D., and Harold H. Kassarjian, (1988), "Consumer Behaviour", Prentice –Hall of India Pvt. Ltd., New Delhi 5th ed.

Carl E. Block & Kenneth J. Roering, (1982), "Essentials of Consumer Behaviour", The Dryden press, Hinsdale, Illionis.

Chester R. Wassan, David H. Mc Conaughy, (1968), "Buying Behaviour and Marketing Decisions," Appleti on–Century–Crofts–New York.

Chisnall, Peter M., (1975), "Marketing–A Behavioural Analysis", McGraw Hill Book Company Limited, London: p.22.

——,(1988), Compton's Encyclopedia and Fact-Index, USA: University of Chicago, Vol.15, p.631.

Cox and Enis, (1969), "Experimentation for Marketing Decisions, International Text Book Company," Scranton, Pennsylvania.

Crisp, Richard D., (1957), "Marketing Research", Mc Graw Hill Book Co., New York.

Crosby, Philip B., (1979), "Quality is Free": "The Art of Making Quality Certain", McGraw-Hill,. New York.

Dalrymple, Douglas J., and Leonard S. Persons, (1983), "Marketing Management- Strategy and Cases", John Wiley and Sons,. New York.

David G. Hughes and Micheal L. Ray, (1974), "Buyer to Consumer Information Processing,", The University of North Corolina Press, Chapel Hill,.

Davis, Kieth and Robert L. Blomstrom, (1975), "Business and Society : Environment and Resposibility", Mc Graw-Hill Inc.,. New York.

Donald F. Cox, (1967), "Risk Handling in Consumer Behaviour – An Intensive Study of Two Cases", "Risk Taking and Information Handling in Consumer Behaviour," Ed., Donald F. Cox, Harward University.

Dororthy Cohen, (1978), "Consumer Behaviour," Random House Business Division, New York.

Edwards W., (1964), "Information Seeking to Reduce the Risk of Decisions", Predecisional Processes in Decision Making: Proceedings of a Symposium, Ohio, wright-Paterson Air Force Base, December, New York.

Elihu Katz and Paul F. Lazars Feld, (1955), "Personal Influence", The Free Press, New York.

Engel James F. & Roger D. Blackwell, (1982), "Consumer Behaviour", Hindale, Dryden Press.

Flemming Hanson, (1972), "Consumer Choice Behaviour: A Cognitive Theory", The Free Press, New York.

Francesco M. Nicosia, (1966), "Consumer Decision processes: Marketing and Advertising Implications," Englewood Cliffs, N.J. Prentice Hall, Inc.,.

Fred D. Reynolds and William D. Wells, (1977), "Consumer Behaviour, "Mc-Graw Hill, New York,. Ghatak, Anita, (1985),

"Consumer Behaviour in India," : D.K. Agencies Pvt. Ltd., New Delhi , 1st ed.

George H. Haines (Jr.), (1969), "Consumer Behaviour-Learning Models of Purchasing," The Free Press, New York.

George Katona, (1960), "The Powerful Consumer", McGraw Hill Book Coy, Inc., New York.

George Katona and Eva Mueller, (1955), "A Study of Purchase Decisions", Consumer Behaviour, Ed., Lincoln H. Clark, , New York University, New York.

Goldmann, Heinz M., (1994), "How to win Customers", Rupa & Co., New Delhi.

Goodstein, Leonard D., and Richard I. Lanyon, (1979), "Adjustment, Behaviour and Personality", Addition–Wesly Publishing Company, London: 2nd ed.

Green, Paul E., Donalld S. Tull and Gerald Albaum, (1995), "Research for Marketing Decisions", Prentice-Hall of India, Pvt., Ltd., New Delhi.

Harold H. Kassarjian and Thomas S. Robertson, (1968), "Percepectives in Consumer Behaviour", Scott, Foresman and company, Glenview, I 11,.

Harper W. Boyd, Ralphh Westfall & Stanley F. Stach, (1988), "Marketing Research Text and Cases," Richard D.Irwin Inc, Illinois., 6th ed.

Harry C.Hansen, (1972), "Marketing : Texts, Cases and Readings", Richard D.Irwin, Inc, Homewood Illinois, New York.

Helmut Becker, (1971), "Consumer Information and the Image of Advertising in Germany with Significant Comparison to America", Unpublished Ph.D. Dissertation, Indiana University.

Howard A. John, (1963), "Marketing Management: Analysis and Planning, "Homewood, I11, Richard D. Irwin, Inc., New York.

Howard A. John, (1977), "Consumer Behaviour", Application Theory, McGraw Hill Book Company, New York.

Howard A. John and Jagdish N. Sheth, (1969), "The Theory of Buyer Behaviour", John Wiley and Sons, New York.

Howard A. John and Lyman E. Ostlund, (1973), "Buyer Behaviours: Theoretical and Empirical Foundations," Alfred A. Knopf, New York.

Howe, Roger J., Dee Gaeddert & Maynard A. Howe, (1993), "Quality on Trial", West Publishing Company, USA.

Jagdish N. Sheth, (1977), "Multivariate Methods for Market and Survey Research", American Marketing Association, Chicago.

Jagdish N. Sheth, (1983), "Research in Marketing", The Research Annual, Jai Press Inc., London, England, Vol. 6.

James F. Engel, David T. Kollat and Roger D. Blackwell, (1980), "Consumer Behaviour", Holt Rinehart and Winston, Inc.. New York.

James H. Nyers & William H. Reynolds, (1967), "Consumer Behaviour and Marketing Management," Houghton Mifflin Company, Boston.

Jerome E. Mc Carthy & Andrew A. Browiz, (1982), "Essentials of Marketing", Revised Edition, Riichard D.Irwin, Inc, Illionis.

Jerome E.AcCarthe & William D.Perreault, (1977), "Basic Marketing : A Managerial Approach", Universal Book Stall, New Delhi, 9th ed.

John O. Shqughnessy, (1987), "Why People buy", Oxford University Press, Inc., New York.

John R.G. Jenkins, (1972), "Marketing and Consumer Behaviour", Pergamon Press, New York.

John Arndt, (1971), "Word-of-Mouth Advertising and Perceived Risk", Prospective in Consumer Behaviour, Ed., Harold H. Kassarjian and Thomas B. Robertson, Glenview, I 11, Scott, Foreman and Company, pp. 330-36.

Joseph F. Hair Jr, Rolph E. Anderson & Ronald L.Tatham, (1990), "Multivariate Data Analysis with Readings" Macmillan, Second Edition, New York.

John R.Evans & Barry Berman, (1990), "Marketing", 4th Edition, Macmillan Public Company, New York.

Kelman H.C. and Coheler, (1959), "Reactions to Persuasive Communication as a Functiuon of Cognitove Needs and Styles", Meeting of Eastern Psychological Association, April, Atlantic City.

Kotharii C.R., (1985)," Research Methodology : Methods and Techniques", Wiley Eastern Limited, New Delhi.

Jagdish N. Sheth, (1983), "Research in Marketing," The Research Annual, Jai Press Inc., London, England, Vol. 6.

Kotler Philip, (1994), "Marketing management", "Analysis, Planning and Implementation and Control", Prentice-Hall of India Pvt. Ltd., New Delhi.

Laura A. Liswood, (1990), "Serving them Right : Innovative & Powerful Customer Retention Strategies", Harper Business, (A Division of Harper & Row Publishers), New York.

Leon G.Schiffman & Ceslie Lazar Kanuk, (1982), "Consumer Behaviour", Prentice Hall of India Private Limited, New Delhi.

Leon G.Schiffman & Ceslie Lazar Kanuk, (1988), "Consumer Behaviour" Third Edition, Prentice Hall of India Private Limited, New Delhi.

Levitt, Theodore, (1986), "The Marketing Imagination", The Free Press, (A Division of Macmillan Inc., New York.

Loudon, David and Albert J. Della Bitta, (2002), "Consumer Behaviour–Concepts and Application," Mc Graw Hill International Edition, New York: (3rd ed), p. 604.

Luck, David J. and Ronald S.Rubin, (1989), "Marketing Research", Prentice-Hall of India Pvt., Ltd., New Delhi.

Mamoria, C.B. and R.L. Joshi, (1979), "Principles and Practice of Marketing in India." Delhi: Kitab Mahal, pp. 94-100.

Majumdar, Ramanuj, (1991), "Marketing Research : Text, Applications and Case Studies", Wiley Eastern Limited, New Delhi.

Micheal A. Anderberg, (1973), "Cluster Analysis For Applications Academic Press," New York.

Mohanty R.K., (1994), "Customer Support Services", in P.K. Sihna and S.C. Sahoo, edt. "Service Marketing Text and Readings", Himalyan Publishing House. Bombay.

Nair, Rajan, (1988), "Marketing," : Sultan Chand & Sons., New Delhi , pp. 243-281.

Paul E. Green, (1968), "Consumer Use of Information", On knowing the Consumer, Ed., Joseph Newman, John Wiley and Sons, Inc., New York.

Paul E. Green and Donald S. Tull, (1973), "Research for Marketing Decisions," Prentice-Hall of India Private Limited, New Delhi.

Paul E. Green & Tull D.S., (1978), "Research for Marketing Decisions", Engelwood Cliffs , Prentice Hall Inc., IV edition , New Jersey.

Payne, Adrain, (1995), "The Essence of Services Marketing", Prentice-hall of India Private Limited, New Delhi.

Peter D.Bennet & Harold H.Kassargian, (1976), "Consumer Behaviour " ,Prentice Hall of India Private Limited, New Delhi.

Peter M. Chisnall, (1975), "Marketing –A Behavioural Analysis," McGraw Hill Book Company, England.

Peters, Thomas J. & Robert H. Waterman Jr., (1982), "In search of Excellence-Lessons from America's Best Run Companies", Harper & Row Publisher inc.,. New York.

Peters Tom & Nancy Austin, (1985), "A Passion for Excellence: Leadership Difference", Warner Books, New York.

Philip Kotler, (1999.), "Marketing Management : Analysis Planning and Control", Engle Wood Cliffs, N.J. Prentice Hall Inc ., New York.

Pillai, R.S.N. and Bagvathi, (1987), "Marketing,", S.Chand & Co., New Delhi : p.297.

Ramanuj Majundar, (1991), "Marketing Research : Text, Application and Case Studies", Wiley Eastern Limited, New Delhi.

Rac, S.L. and I. Natarajan, (1994) ,"Markets for Consumer Products in India", National Council of Applied Economic Research, New Delhi.

Raymond A. Bauer, (1960), "Consumer Behaviour as Risk Taking", Dynamic Marketing For a Changing World, ed., Robert S. Hancock, American Marketing Association, Chicago.

Richard D.Crisp, (1957), "Marketing Research," McGraw-Hill Book Company, New York.

Robert Bartles, (1966), "The Developing of Marketing Thought," Homewood, Ill, Richard D Irwin, Inc., New York.

Robert Feber, (1974), "Handbook of Marketing Research," McGraw Hill Book Company., New York.

Schiffman, Leon G. and Leslie Lazar Kanuk, (1990), "Consumer Behaviour," Prentice – Hall of India Private Limited, NewDelhi: 3rd ed., p.67.

Scoot Ward & Thomas S.Robertson, (1973), "Consumer Behaviour: Theoretical Sources," Prentice Hall, Inc. Engle Wood Cliffs, NewJersey.

Stanton, William J., (1990), "Fundamentals of Marketing",. McGraw Hill, New York, 3rd ed.

Subroto Sengupta, (1990), "Brand Positioning Strategies for Competitive Advantages", : TaTa McGraw Hill Book Publishing Limited, New Delhi.

——,The New Encyclopedia Britannica USA : University of Chicago, Vol. 8, p. 367.

Thomas C.Kinnear & James R. Taylor, (1983), "Marketing Research: An Apllied Approach", I.S.Eds McGraw Hill, Kugakusha, Limited, Tokyo.

Tulving, Endel, (1972), Episodic and Semantic Memory, in Endel Tulving and W. Donaldson, Eds. Organization of Memory, New York: Academic Press. pp.381-403.

Vithala R.Rao, (1982), "Conjoint Measurement in Marketing Analysis, Multivariate Methods for Market and Survey Research".

William M.Weilbacher, (1967), "Advertising," Macmillan Publishing Company, Second Edition, Boston.

William W. Cooley, Paul R.Lohnes, (1971), Multivariate Data Analysis, John Wiley & Sons Inc. New York.

Wroe Alderson, (1957), "Marketing Behaviour and Executive Action", Homewood, Ill, Richard D. Irwin, Inc., New York.

JOURNAL

Akshay R.Rao & kent B. Monroe, (1989), "The Effect of Price, Brand Name and Store Name on Buyers Perceptions of Product Quality : An Integrated Review", Journal of Marketing Research, August, Vol. 26, pp. 351-357.

Alan Resnik & Bruce L. Stern, (1977), "An Analysis of Information Content in Television Advertising", Journal of marketing, January, pp. 50-53.

Albert R. Wildt, Albert V. Bruno & James L. Ginter, (1981), "Attitude Models", Journal of Advertising Research, August, Vol. 21, No.4, pp. 61-70.

Anderson, C.D and J.K. Claxton, (1982), "Preference Group Influence on Product and Brand Purchase Decisions", Journal of Consumer Research, (September). Vol. 9 (2).

Anthony, Bushman F., (1982), "Systamatic Life Styles for New Product Segmentation", Journal of the Academy of Marketing Science, Vol.10 (4), pp. 377-394.

Arun K. Jain & Michael Etgar, "Measuring Store Image Through Multidimensional Scaling of Free Response Data" Vol. 52, No.4, pp. 61-79.

Atif Mohamed H., (1977), "Consumer Protection in Underdeveloped Countries", *Indian Journal of Marketing,* September, Vol. No.1, pp. 3-9.

Bahl, Sushil, (1991), "The Customer As Partner", Business World, 30th Jan.–12th Feb p.19.

Barkstak and French A., (1976), "The Response of US Business to Consumerism", *European Journal of Marketing*, Vol.10, No.1, pp.13-27.

Bayus, Barry L. (1991), "The Consumer Durable Replacement Buyer", *Journal of Marketing, January,* Vol.55, pp. 42-50.

Bearden, William O. and Etzel Micheal J., (1982) "Reference Group Influence on Produce and Brand Purchase Decisions", *Journal of Consumer Research,* September , Vol.9, No.2, pp. 13-194.

Bennett, P.D. and R.M. Mandell, (1969), "Per-purchase Information Seeking Behaviour of New Car Purchasers – The Learning Hypothesis," *Journal of Marketing Research,* (November), Vol. VI, pp. 430-433.

Bent Stidson, (1970), "Some Thoughts on the Advertising Process", *Journal of Marketing,* January, Vol. 34 pp. 47-53.

Berning, Carol Kohn and Jacob Jacohy, (1974), "Patterns of Information Acquistion in New Product Purchase, *Journal of Consumer Research,*" (September), Vol. 1, p. 22.

Bettman, James R., (1971), "The Structure of Consumer Choice Processes, *Journal of Marketing Research,*" (November), Vol. 8(4), pp. 465-71.

Bettman, James R. and Park C.Whan, (1980), "Effects of Prior Knowledge and Experience and Phase of the Choice Process on Consumer Decision Process: A Protocol Analysis," *Journal of Consumer Research,* Vol. 77, pp. 234 – 284.

Bhan, K.D., (1986), "How and When do Brand Perceptions and Preferences First Form? A Congnitives Development Investigation," *Journal of Consumer Research,* (December) Vol. 13 (3).

Bloom, Paul and Ford Gary T., (1979), "Evaluation of Consumer Education Progress", *Journal of Consumer Research,* December, Vol.6, No.3, pp. 270-79.

Bogart, Leo and Charles Lehman, (1973), "What Makes A Brand Name Familiar", *Journal of Marketing Research,* Vol. X, pp. 17-22.

Bonfield E.H., (1974), "Attitudes, Social Influence, Personal Norm and Intention Interactions as Related to Brand Purchase Behaviour" *Journal of Marketing,* November, Vol. 9 pp. 379-389.

Boyd H.W. & Levy Sidney, (1963), "New Dimensions in Consumer Analysis", Harvard Business Review, November–December, pp. 129-140.

Brucks, Marrie, (1985), "The Effects of Product Class Knowledge on Information Search Behaviour," *Journal of Consumer Research* June , Vol.12, pp. 1-16.

Capon, N. and D. Kuhn (1982), "Can Consumers Calculate Best Buys?," *Journal of Consumer Research,* March, Vol. 8 (4) p. 80.

Chester R.Wasson, "Common Sense in Sampling", Harvard Business Review, pp. 109-114.

Clarke, Y. and G.N. Soutar, (1982), "Consumers Acquisition Patterns for Durable Goods: Australian Evidence," *Journal of Consumer Research,* March, Vol.8 (4), p.110.

Claxton, John D., Joseph N. Fry and Bernard Portis, (1974) : "A Taxonomy of Pre-Purchase Information Gathering Patterns," *Journal of Consumer Research,* December,Vol. 1. pp. 35-42.

Cosenza, Robert, (1985), "Family Decision Making, Decision Dominance Structure Analysis–An Extension," *Journal of the Academy of Marketing Science,* Vol. 13 (1), pp. 91-103.

Cox, W.E. Jr. and E.F.Cooke, (1970), "Other Dimensions Involved in Shopping Centre Preference," *Journal of Marketing,* October, Vol. 34(4), pp. 12-17.

Crites, Dennis M., John A.Shaw and Sak Onkvisit, (1979), "Information Source Usage by Prospective Home Buying Consumers *Journal of the Academy of Marketing Science.* "Vol.7, (2), pp. 80-94.

Crosby, Lawrence, Taylor and James, (1981), "Effects of Consumer Information and Education on Cognition and Choice", *Journal of Consumer Research,* 1981,Vol. 8, No.1, pp.43-56.

Dan Sarel, (1983),"A Comment on Capon and Lutz Model and Methodology for the Development of Consumer Information

Programmes", *Journal of Consumer Research,* Summer , Vol. 47, pp.103-107.

David A. Aaker & Donald Norris, (1982), "Characteristics of T.V. Commercials Perceived as Informative", *Journal of Advertising Research,* April/May, Vol. 22, 2 pp. 61- 70.

Davies R.L., (1973), "Evaluation of Retail Store Attributes and Sales Performance" European *Journal of Marketing,* Vol. 7, No. 2, pp. 89-102.

Day, George S & David A. Aakar, (1970), "A Guide to Consumerism", *Journal of Marketing,* July Vol. 34.

Debra L. Scammon, (1977), "Information Load and Consumers", *Journal of Consumer Research,* December, Vol.4, No. 3, pp.148-155.

Dennis L.Rosen, Richard W. Olshavsky, (1987), "A Protocol Analysis of Brand Choice Strategies Involving Recommendations", *Journal of Consumer Research,* June, Vol. 14, pp.440-444.

Dilip Thakore, (1980), "Consumer Marketing: The Disorientation of the Consumers", Indian *Journal of Marketing,* February, Vol. No.6, pp.29-32.

Dommermuth W.P., (1965), "The Shopping Matrix and Marketing Strategy", *Journal of Marketing Research,* May, Vol.11, pp.128-132.

Dommermuth, William P., (1965), "The Shopping Matrix and Marketing Strategy", *Journal of Marketing Research,* May, pp. 128-132.

Don L.Coursey, (1988), "Preference Trees, Preference Hierarchies and Consumer Behaviour", *Journal of consumer Research,* December, Vol.1.

Donald G. Marrision, (1969), "On the Interpretation of Discriminant Analysis", *Journal of Marketing Research,* May (6), pp. 156-163.

Donald G.Morrision, (1979), "Purchase Intentions and Purchase Behaviour", *Journal of Marketing,* Vol. 43, Spring, pp. 65-74.

Donald J. Hempel, (1966), "An Experimental Study of the Efforts of Information on Consumer Product Evaluation", Science, Technology and Marketing, American Marketing Association, pp. 51-71.

Donald R. Lehmann, (1971), "Television Show Preference: Application of a Choice Model" *Journal of Marketing Research,* February, Vol. 8, pp. 47-55.

Dunsing, Marilyn M. and Jeanne L. Haftstrom, (1975), "Methodological Consideration in Family Decision Making Studies," *Advances in Consumer Research,* Vol. 2, p. 172.

Edward J. Russo, (1974), "More Information is Better : A Re-evaluation of Jacoby, Speller and Kohn", *Journal of Consumer Research,* December, Vol.1, pp.68-72.

Edward Russo L. & Erick J.Johnson, (1980), "What Do Consumers Know About Familiar Products", *Advances in Consumer in Consumer Research"*, Vol. 7, pp. 417-423.

Eli Seggy, (1970), "Brand Assortment and Consumer Brand Choice", *Journal of Marketing,* October , Vol. 34, pp.18-24.

Ernest Dichter, (1966), "How Word–of –Mouth Advertising Works", *Harvard Business review,* November–December , pp. 149-166.

Evrard, Yues, (1982), "Multivariate Data Analysis and Consumer Behaviour : A Review", Esomar Congress, Vienna, August – September , Vol.11 pp. 211-28.

Ferber, R., and L.C. Lee, (1974), "Husband Wife Influence in Family Purchasing Behaviour," *Journal of Consumer Research,* June, pp. 43-50.

Filia Trault, P., and J.R.B. Ritchie, (1980), "Joint Purchasing Decision –A Comparison of Influence Structure in Family, and Couple Decision Making Units", *Journal of Consumer Research,* September, Vol. 7(2), pp. 131-140.

Fleming Hanson, (1976), "Psychological Theories of Consumer Choice", *Journal of Consumer Research,* December, Vol.3, pp.133.

Francis X. Callaham, (1974), "Advertising Influence of Consumer's", *Journal of Adverising Research,* June, Vol. 14,No.3, pp.45-48.

Fred D. Reynolds and Willian R. Darden, (1971), "Mutually Adaptive Effects of Inter-personal Communication", *Journal of Marketing Research,* November, Vol.8, pp. 449-54.

Frederic B.Kraft & Donald H. Granbois, (1973), "Brand Evaluation and Brand Choice", *Journal of Marketing Research,* August, Vol. 10, pp.235-241.

Freuden, Jon B. and Douglas S. Bible, (1982), "The Home Purchase Process: Measurement of Evaluative Criteria Through

Pairwise Measures", Journal of the Academy of Marketing Science, Vol. 10(4), (Fall), pp. 359-376.

Fry, J.N., and F.H. Siller, (1970), "A Comparison of House Wife Decision Making in Two Social Classes ", (August), Vol. 7(3), pp. 333-337.

Gary M. Erickson & Johny K. Johansson, (1985), "The Role of Price in Multi–Attribute Product Evaluations", *Journal of Consumer Research,* September, Vol. 12, pp. 195-197.

Gary T. Ford & Ruth Ann Smith, (1987), "Inferential Beliefs in Consumer Evaluations : An Assessment of Alternative Processing Strategies", *Journal of Consumer Research,* December, Vol. 14, pp. 363-371.

Gerald J. Tellis, "Consumer Purchasing Strategies and the Information in Retail Prices", *Journal of Retailing,* Vol. 63, Fall, pp. 279-297.

Gerald J. Tellis & Gary J. Gaeth, (1990), "Best Value, Price Seeking and price Aversion : The Impact of Information and Learning On Consumer Choices", *Journal of Marketing,* Vol. 54, pp. 34-45.

Geraldini Fennel, (1978), "Consumers Perceptions of The Product–Use Situation", *Journal of Marketing,* April, Vol. 42, pp. 38-47.

George P. Moschis, (1976), "Shopping Orientation and Customer Uses of Information", *Journal of Retailing,* Vol. 52, No 2, Summer, pp.61-70.

George S. Day and David A. Aaker, (1970), "A Guide to Consumerism", *Journal of Marketing,* July, Vol.34, pp.12-19.

Gert Assumus, (1977), "Evolution Changes in the Marketing Information System", European *Journal of Marketing,* Vol. II, No.4, pp. 272-280.

Gilani, J., "Role of Advertising in India", *Indian Journal of Marketing,* pp. 26 –31.

Ginter, J.L., (1974), "An Experimental Investigation of Attitude Change and Choice of New Brand", *Journal of Marketing Research,* Vol. 11, pp. 30-40.

Girish Punj & David W. Steward, (1983), "Cluster Analysis in Marketing Research : Review and Suggestions for Application", *Journal of Marketing Research,* Vol. 20, pp. 135.

Granger C.W.J. and Billlson A., (1972), "Consumer Attitude Towards Package, Size and Price", *Journal of Marketing Research,* August, Vol. IX, pp. 239-248.

Hans B. Thorelli, (1971), "Concentration of Information Power Among Consumers", *Journal of Marketing Research,* November, Vol. VIII, pp. 427-432.

Hans B. Thorelli and Jack L. Engeldow, (1980), "Information Seekers and Information Systems : A Policy Perspective", *Journal of Marketing,* Vol. 44, Spring, pp. 9-27.

Harold H. Kassarjian, (1977), "Content Analysis in Consumer Behaviour", *Journal of Consumer Research,* June, Vol.4, pp. 8-18.

Hary C.Triandis, (1964), "Exploring Factor Analyses of The Behavioural Component of Social Attitudes", *Journal of Abnormal and Social Psychology,* Vol. 168, No 4, pp. 420-430.

Heisley, Deborah D. and Paula S. Holmes, (1987), "A Review of Family Consumption Research–The Need for a More Anthropological Perspective", Advances in Consumer Research, Vol. XIV.

Helgeson, J.G. et.al., (1984), "Trends in Consumer Behaviour Literature: A Content Analysis", *Journal of Consumer Research,* (March), Vol. 10 (4).

Hempel, Donald J., (1975), "Family Role Structure and Housing Decisions, Advances in Consumer Research", Vol.2, pp. 71-80.

Hill, Ronald P. and Mery I.P. Gardner, (1987), "The Buying Process: Effects of and on Consumer Mood Status, Advances in Consumer Research", Vol. XIV, p. 435.

Hiram C. Barksdale and William R.Darden, (1972), "Consumer Behaviour", *Journal of Marketing,* October, Vol. 36, pp. 28- 35.

Huber, Joel and Andrew L. Czajka, (1981), "Modeling Buy/No Buy Decisions: A Comparision of Two Methods", Advances in Consumer Research, Vol. IX.

Hundal B.S. and H.S. Sandhu, (1987), "Buyer Behaviour of Television Buyers in Punjab – A Case Study," *Indian Journal of Marketing,* Vol. XVIII (2-4), (October-December) New Delhi: pp. 23-28.

Hutton, R.B. et.al., (1986), "Effects of Cost Related Feedback on Consumer Knowledge and Consumption Behaviour: A Field

Experimental Approach", *Journal of Consumers Research,* (December), Vol. 13 (3).

Ian Fenwick, (1980), "A User's Guide to Conjoint Measurement in Marketing ", European *Journal of Marketing,* Vol. 12, pp. 203-211.

Iyer, Easwar, (1987), "Deviations from a Shopping Plan: When and Why do Consumers Not Buy Items as Planned," Advances in Consumer Research, Vol. XIV, pp. 246-250.

Jack Abrams, (1966), "An Evaluation of Alternative Rating Devices for Consumer Research", *Journal of Marketing Research,* May, Vol. 3, pp.189-193.

Jacob Jacoby, Donald E. Speller, Carolkohn Bernning, (1974), "Brand Choice Behaviour As a Function of Information Load: Replication and Extension", *Journal of Consumer Research,* June, Vol. 1, pp. 33-42.

Jagdish N. Sheth, (1970), "Multivatiate Analysis in Marketing", *Journal of Advertising Research,* February, Vol. 10, No.1, pp. 29-39.

Jagdish N. Sheth, (1979), "How Consumer Use Information", European Research, July, Vol. 7, No.4, pp. 167-173.

James F. Engel, Roger D. Blackwell and Robert J. Kegerrs, (1969), "How Information is Used tc Adopt an Innovation", *Journal of Adversing Research,* Vol. 9, No. 4, pp. 3-8.

James R. Bettman, (1975), "Issues in Designing Consumer Information Environments", *Journal of Consumer Research,* December, Vol. 2, pp. 169-177.

James R. Bettman, (1973), "Perceived Risk and It's Components: A Model and Empirical Test", *Journal of Marketing Research,* May, Vol. 10, 1973, pp.184-190.

James R. Bettman & Jacob Jacby, (1976), "Patterns of Processing In Consumer Information Acquisition", Advances in Consumer Research, Vol. 3, pp. 315-320.

James W. Taylor, (1974), "The Role of Risk in consumer Behaviour", *Journal of Marketing,* April,Vol. 38, pp. 54-60.

Jan-Benedict E., & M. Steekamp, (1991), "Segmenting Retail Markets on Store Image Using a Customer Based Methodology", *Journal of Retailing,* Vol. 67, No 3, Fall pp. 300-319.

Jeffrey A. Barach, (1969), "Advertising Effectiveness and Risk In Consumer Decision Process", *Journal of Marketing Research,* August, Vol. 6, pp. 214-220.

Jerome B. Kernan, (1987), "Chasing The Holy Grail : Reflections on "What is consumer Research", *Journal of Consumer Research,* June, Vol. 14, pp. 133-135.

Joan Meyers–Levy, (1989), "The Influence of a Brand Name's Association Set Size and Word Frequency on Brand Memory", *Journal of Consumer Research,* September, Vol. 16, pp. 197-207.

Joel E.Urbany, Peter R. Dickson & William L. Wilkie, (1989), "Buyers Uncertainty And Information Search", *Journal of Consumer Research,* September Vol. 16, pp. 208-215.

Johan Arndt & Edgar Crane, (1975), "Observing Stages In Consumer Decision Processes", Advances in Consumer Research, Schilinger Mary Jane edn. Vol. 2, 1975, pp. 63-70.

John A. Howard, (1987), "Buyer Behavior and Related Technological Advances", *Journal of Consumer Research,* December, Vol. 14, pp. 363-371.

John Arndt, (1967), "Role of Product-Related Conversation in the Diffusion of a New Product", *Journal of Marketing Research,* August, pp. 291-95.

John D. Claxton, Joseph N. Fry, Bernard Portis, (1974), "A Taxonomy of Pre-purchase Information Gathering Patterns", *Journal of Consumer Research,* December, Vol.1, pp. 35-42.

John D. Claxton, Ritchie, Brent and Zaichokowsky Judy, (1980), "The Normal Group Technique: It potential for Consumer Research", *Journal of Consumer Research,* December, Vol. 7, No. 3, pp. 308-313.

John, D.R. and C.A. Cole, (1986)," Age Differences in Information Processing : Understanding Deficits in Young and Elderly Consumers", *Journals of Consumer Research,* (December), Vol. 13 (3).

John H. Murphy & Kenneth A. Coney, (1975), "Comments on Consumer Store Images and Store Loyalties", *Journal of Marketing,* July, Vol. 39, pp. 64-66.

John Watson, (1982), "Interview Today's Customer-Tomorrow", *Journal of Advertising Research,* Vol. 22, No.5, pp.17-23.

John willing and Bauer A. Raymond, (1968), "Consumer Goals and Reactions to a Communication Source", *Journal of Advertising Research,* February, Vol.5, pp. 73-77.

Jonathan Gutman, (1982), "The Impact of Advertising at the Time of Consumption", *Journal of Advertising Research,* Vol. 22, No.4, pp.35-42.

Joseph F.Dash, Leon G.Schiffman and Conrad Berenson, (1976), "Information Search and Store Choice", *Journal of Advertising Research,* June, Vol. 16, No. 3, pp. 35-40.

Joseph W. Newmann and Bradley D. Lockman, (1975), "Measuring Pre-purchase Information Seeking", *Journal of Consumer Research,* December 21, pp. 216-222.

Joseph W.Newmann and Richard Staelin, (1971), "Multivative Analysis of Differences in Buyer Decision Time", *Journal of Marketing Research,* May, Vol. VIII, pp. 192-199.

Joseph W. Newmann and Richard Staelin, (1972), "Pre-purchase Information Seeking for New Cars and Major Household Appliances", *Journal of Marketing Research,* August, Vol. (9), pp. 249-57.

Joseph W. Newmann and Richard Staelin, (1973), "Information Sources of Durable Goods", *Journal of Advertising Research,* April, Vol. 134,No.2, pp. 19-29.

Joseph F.Dash, Leon G.Sciffman and Conrad Berenson, (1976), "Information Search and Store Choice", *Journal of Advertising Research,* June, Vol. 16, pp.35-40.

Joseph F.Dash, Leon G. Sciffman & Conrad Berenson, (1976), "Risk and Personality Related Dimensions of Store Choice", *Journal of Marketing, January,* Vol. 40, pp. 32-39.

Joseph F.Hair , Jr., Rolph E.Anderson & Ronald L.Tatham, (1990), "Multivariate Data Analysis With Readings", Macmillian, Newyork, Second Edition, pp. 302.

Joseph W.Newman & Richard A.Werbal, (1973), "Multivariate Analysis of Brand Loyalty for Major Household Appliances", *Journal of Marketing Research,* November, Vol. 8, pp.404-409.

Joseph W.Newman & Ricard Staelin, (1972), "Pre-purchase Information Seeking For New Cars and Major Household Appliances', *Journal of Marketing Research,* August, Vol. 9, pp. 249-257.

Kaleem Mohammad Kahn, (1988), "The Study of Reference Groups in Influencing Purchase Situations : Need For Multiple Research Orientations", Marketology, July–September, pp. 29-32.

Kehret–Ward, T. and R. Yalch, (1984), "To Take or Not to Take the Only One: Effects of Changing the Meaning of a Product Attribute on Choice Behaviour", *Journal of Consumer Research,* March, Vol. 10 (4).

Keith Bryant, (1988), "Durable and Wife's Employment Yet Again", *Journal of Consumer Research,* June,Vol. 15, pp.195-199.

Kevin Lane Keller & Richard Stealin, (1987), "Effects of Quality and Quantity of Information on Decision Effectiveness", *Journal of Consumer Research,* September, Vol. 14, pp. 200-213.

Kollat, David T., James F. Engel and Roger D. Black Well; (1970), "Current Problems in Consumer Behaviour Research", *Journal of Marketing Research,* August, Vol. 7(3), pp. 327-332.

Kyle Peter W., (1982), "The Impact of Advertising on Markets", *Journal of Advertising,* October–December, Vol.1, No.4, pp. 345-59.

Lambert, Zarre V., (1972), "Price and Choice Behaviour", *Journal or Marketing Research,* February, Vol. IX(1), pp. 35-40.

Lantus Geofrey P., (1982), "An Improved Research Methodology for Studying Consumer Information Processing Behaviour", *Journal of Market Research Society,* January, Vol. 24, No.1, pp.29-45.

Laurel Anderson, Huddson & Julie L. Ozenne, (1983), "Alternative ways of Seeking Knowledge in Consumer Research", *Journal of Consumer Research* March, Vol. 15, pp. 508-521.

Lavidge R.J. & Steiner G.A., (1961), "A Model for Predicting Measurement of Advertising Effectiveness", *Journal of Marketing,* Vol. 25, pp. 59-62.

Le Grand, Bruce and John G. Udell, (1964), "Consumer Behaviour In The Market Place-An Empirical study In The Television and Furniture Fields with Theoretical Implications", *Journal of Retailing,* Vol. 40, Fall p. 32.

Louis L. Stern, (1967), "Consumer Protection Via Increased Information", *Journal of Marketing,* April, Vol. 31, pp. 48-52.

Malhotra, Naresh K., (1984), "Reflections on the Information Overload Paradign in Consumer, Decision Making", *Journal of Consumer Research,* (March 10), pp. 436-40.

Malhotra, Naresh K. Arun K. Jain, and Stephen W.Lagakos, (1982), "The Information Overload Controversy: An Alternative Viewpoint", *Journal of Marketing,* Vol. 46 (2), (Spring), pp. 27-37.

Markin, Rom J., (1979), "The Role of Rationalisation in Consumer Decision Making Process: A Revisionist Approach", *Journal of the Academy of Marketing's Science.* Vol. 7(4). (Fall) pp. 316.

Micheal Perry, (1969), "Discriminant Analysis of Relations Between Consumer's Attitudes, Behaviour and Intentions", *Journal of Advertising Research,* June, Vol. 9, No. 2.

Michael B. Meansco & David J. Furry, (1989), "Utility and Choice: An Empirical Study of Wife/Husband Decision Making", *Journal of Consumer Research,* June, Vol. 16, pp. 87-97.

Mita, Sujan, (1985), "Consumer Knowledge : Effects on Evaluation Strategies Mediating Consumer Judgement", *Journal of Consumer Research,* Vol.12 (1), pp. 31-46.

Narasimhan and Srinivasan, (1987), "A Path Analytic Model of External Search for Information for New Automobiles advances in Consumer Research", Vol. XIV, pp. 319-322.

Neil H. Borden, (1964), "The Concept of Marketing Mix", *Journal of Advertising Research,* March, Vol. 4, No.1, pp. 2-7.

Nelson, Philip, (1970), "Information and Consumer Behaviour", *Journal of Political Economy,* (March/April), Vol. 78, pp. 311-329.

Newman, J.W. and R. Staelin, (1972), "Pre-purchase Information Seeking for New Cars and Major Household Appliances", *Journal of Marketing Research,* (August), Vol. IX, pp. 269-275.

Noel Capon and Richard J. Lutz, (1979), "A Model and Methodology for the Development of Consumer Information Programmes", *Journal of Marketing,* January, Vol. 43, pp. 58-67.

Noel Capon and Richard J. Lutz, (1983), "The Marketing of Consumer Information", *Journal of Marketing,* Summer, Vol. 47, pp. 108-112.

Noreen M. Klein & Manjit S. Yadav, (1989), "Context Effects on Effort and Accuracy in Choice : An Enquiry in to Adaptive Decision Making", *Journal of Consumer Research,* March , Vol. 15, pp. 411-421.

O'Brien, Terrence Vol., (1977), "Information Handling in Consumers Decisions", *Journal of the Academy of Marketing Science,* Vol. 5(2), pp. 230-232.

O'Brien, Terrence, (1977), "Informational Handling in Consumer Decisions of the Academy of Marketing Science",Vol. 5 (3), (Summer), pp. 229-232.

Palachek, Albrt D and Kerin, Roger No, (1982), "Alternative Approaches to the Two Group Concordance Problem in Brand Preference Ranking", *Journal of Marketing Research,* August, Vol. XIX, No.3, pp. 386-89.

Park C. Whan, (1978), "A Few Question on Consumer Information Processing: Two Product Cases–Coffee and Toothpaste", *Journal of Marketing Research,* May, Vol.XV, No.2, pp.243-49.

Park, Whan , C., Lessig, V. Parker and James R. Merrill, (1981),"The Elusive Role of Price in Brand Choice Behaviour", Advances in Consumer Reseach, Vol. IX.

Parker, Lessig V. and Beverlee B. Anderson, (1974), "Do Different Consumers Operate Under the Same Preference Model", *Journal of the Academy of Marketing Science,* Vol.4(1), (Winter), pp. 357-366.

Parker, Lessig V. and Thomas P. Copley, (1974), "Consumer Beliefs, Attitudes and Brand Preferences", *Journal of the Academy of Marketing Science,* Vol. 2 (2), (Spring), pp. 184-188.

Paul E.Green, Abba M. Krieger & Monoj K.Agarwal, (1991), "Adaptive Conjoint Analysis: Some Caveats and Suggestions", *Journal of Marketing Research,* May, Vol. 28, pp. 215-222.

Paul E., Green, Micheal N. Halbert, and J. Sayer Minas, (1964), "An Experiment In Information Buying", *Journal of Advertising Research,* September, Vol. 4, No.3, pp.17-23.

Paul E. Green and Srinivasan V., (1978), "Conjoint Analysis in Consumer Research: Issues and Outlook", *Journal of Consumer Research, September,* Vol.5, pp. 103-123.

Paul E. Green & Stewart W. Bither, (1991), "Segmenting Markets with Conjoint Analysis", *Journal of Marketing,* Vol. 55, pp. 20-31.

Paul, Peter J. and Michael J. Ryan, (1976), "An Investigation of Perceived Risk at the Brand Level", *Journal of Marketing Research,* May, Vol. XIII(2) mpp. 184-188.

Pickering J.F., "Verbal Explanations of Consuemr Durable Purchase Decisions", *Journal of the Market Research Society,* Vol. 17, No 2.

Prakash Nedungadi, (1990), "Recall and Consideration Sets: Influencing Choice Without Altering Brand Evaluations", *Journal of Consumer Research,* December , Vol. 17, pp.263-276.

Qualls, William J., (1981), "Changing Sex Roles : Its Impact Upon Family Decision Making" Advances in Consumer Research, Provo : Association for Consumer Research, Vol. IX, pp. 267-270.

Rao, Vithala R., (1972), "Changes in Explicit Information and Brand Perceptions", *Journal of Marketing Research,* May, Vol. IX, pp. 209-273.

Rashi Glazer, (1984), "Multi-attribute Perceptual Bias as Revealing of Preference Structure", *Journal of Consumer Research,* June, Vol.11, pp. 510-521.

Ratchford, Brain T., (1980), "The Value of Information for Selected Appliance's", *Journal of Marketing Research,* February, Vol. XVII (1), pp. 14-25.

Rayan, M.J., (1982), "Behavioural Intention Formation : The Inter Dependency of Attitudinel and Social Influence Variables", *Journal of Consumer Research,* December, Vol. 9 (3).

Richard J. Lutz & Patrick J. Reily, (1974), "An Exploration of the Effects of Perceived Social and Performance Risk on Consumer Information Acquisition", Advances in Consumer Research, Scotward and Peter Wright edn., Vol. 1, pp. 393-405.

Richard N. Farmer, (1967), "Would You Want Your Daughter to Marry a Marketing Man?", *Journal of Marketing,* January, Vol.31, pp.3-7.

Richard Staelin, (1978), "The Effects of Consumer Education on Consumer Product Safety Behaviour", *Journal of Consumer Research,* June, Vol.5, No.1, pp. 30-40.

Rites C.B., (1996-67), "What Influences Purchase of Colour Television", *Journal of Retailing,* 42, Winter, pp.25-31.

Robert A. Westbrook and Class Fornell, (1979), "Patterns of Information Sources Usage Among Durable Goods Buyer", *Journal of Marketing Research,* August, Vol. 26, pp.303-312.

Robert B. Settle, (1972), "Attribution Theory and Acceptance of Information", *Journal of Marketing Research,* February, Vol. IX, pp. 85-88.

Robert B. Woodruff, (1972), "Brand Information Sources, Opinion Change and Uncertainity", *Journal of Marketing Research,* November, Vol. IX, pp.414-418.

Robert B. Woodruff, (1972), "Measurement of Consumer's Prior Brand Information", *Journal of Marketing Research,* August (9), pp. 258-263.

Robert E. Smith and William R. Swinayard, (1983), "Attitude Behaviour Consistency: The Impact of Product Trail Vs Advertising", *Journal of Marketing Research,* August, Vol.20, pp. 257-67.

Robert, Kelly F., (1968), "The Search Correspondent of the Consumer Decision Process-A Theoretic Examination, Marketing and The New Science of Planning", Chicago: American Marketing Association, p. 273.

Roering, Kenneth J. and Carl E. Block, (1976), "Population Density and Type of Purchase of Explanatory Variable in Consumer Information Search", *Journal of the Academy of Marketing Science* Vol.4 (4), (Fall), pp.731-74.

Rudd, J., and F.J. Kohout, (1983), "Individual and Group Consumer Information Acquisition in Brand Choice Situation", *Journal of Consumer Research,* December, Vol. (3).

Rustom S. Daver, "What Makes the Consumer Tick? Application of Maslow's Hierarchy Concept to Customer Motivation", *Indian Journal of Marketing,* p. 21.

Sahu G.N., (1981), "Consumer Problems in India", *Indian Journal of Marketing,* May, Vol. 9, No.11, pp. 3-8.

Saunders J.A., "Cluster Analysis for Market Segmentation", *European Journal of Marketing,* Vol. 14, 7, p. 425.

Schaninger, C.M. and C.T. Allen, (1981), "Wife's Occupational Status as a Consumer Behaviour Construct", *Journal of Consumer Research,* September, Vol. 8 (2).

Sengupta, Subroto, (1990), "Brand Positioning-Strategies for Competitive Advantage", New Delhi: Tata McGraw Hill Book Publishing Company Ltd., pp. 222-23.

Settle, Robert B., (1972), "Attribution Theory and Acceptance of Information", *Journal of Marketing Research,* February, Vol. IX (1), pp. 85-88.

Spiro, R.L., (1983), "Persuasion in Family Decision–Making", *Journal of Consumer Research,* (March) , Vol. 9 (4), p.

Srinivasan, T.C., (1987), "An Integrated Approach to Consumer Choice", Advances in Consumer Research, Vol. XIV (I), pp. 96-100.

Srull, Thomas K., (1987), "Memory, Mood, and Consumer Judgement", Advances in Consumer Research, Vol. XIV, p.404.

S'Brien, Terrence V., (1971), "Tracking Consumer Decision Making", *Journal of Marketing,* January, Vol. 35 (1), pp. 34-40.

Stem, Jr., D.E., C.W.Lamp & D.L.Mac Lachlan, (1979), "Perceived Risk": A Synthesis", *European Journal of Marketing,* Vol. 11, No 4, pp. 312-319.

Tan, Chin Tiong and Ira J. Dolich, (1983), "A Comparative Study of Consumer Information Seeking: Singapore Vs. U.S., *Journal of the Academy of Marketing Science*", Vol.11 (3), pp. 313-322.

Ted Roselius, (1971), "Consumer Rankings of Risk Reduction Methods", *Journal of Marketing Research,* January, Vol. 35, pp. 56-61.

Thomas J.Reynolds & James P. Jolly, "Measuring Personal Values: An Evaluation of Alternative Methods", pp. 531-536.

Thorelli, Hans B. and Jack L. Engledow, (1980), "Information Seekers and Information System: A Policy Prospective", *Journal of Marketing,* Vol. 44 (2). (Spring). pp. 9-27.

Thorelli, H.B., (1971), "Concentration of Information Power Among Consumers", *Journal of Marketing Research,* (November), Vol.8 (4), pp.427-432.

Turnbull P.W. & A.Meenaghan, "Diffusion of Innovation and Opinion Leadership", *European Journal of Marketing,* Vol. 14, No 1, pp. 3-28.

Udell, J.G., (1966), "Pre-purchase Behaviour of Buyers of Small electrical Appliances", *Journal of Marketing,* October, Vol. 30, pp. 50-52.

Ustle, Glenn and Ryans John K., (1981), "Techniques for Measuring Advertising Effectiveness", *Journal of Advertising Research,* June, Vol.21, No.3, pp. 19-22.

Valerie S. Folkes, (1988), "The Availability of Heuristic and Perceived Risk", *Journal of Consumer Research,* June, Vol. 15, pp.13-22.

Walter A. Woods (1960), "Psychological Dimensions of Consumer Decision", *Journal of Marketing,* January, pp.15-19.

Walters, Glenn C., (1979), "Consumer Behaviour: An Appraisal", *Journal of the Academy of Marketing Science,* Vol.7(4), pp. 273-284.

Wasson, Chester R., (1979), "Consumer Choice Process Search or Automatic Responses.", *Journal of the Academy of Marketing Science,* Vol. 7 (4), (Fall), pp. 360-373).

Wesley Hutchison J. & Joseph W. Alba, (1991), "Ignoring Irrelevant Information: Situational Determinants of Consumer Learning", *Journal of Consumer Research,* December, Vol. 18, pp. 325-345.

West Brook, R.A, and C.Fornell, (1979), "Patterns of Information Source Usage Among Durable Goods Buyers", *Journal of Marketing Research,* August Vol. XVI, pp. 303-312.

Wheeler, David R., (1974),"Brand Loyaltiess : Qualitative Quantitative or Both", *Journal of the Academy of Marketing Science,* Vol. 2 (2), (Fall), pp. 651-657.

Wiley, James B., (1984), "Toward Upgrading the Quality of Consumer Decision Making", *Journal of the Academy of Marketing Science,* Vol.12(1,2), pp. 1-10.

Wilk, Richard R., (1987), "House, Home and Consumer Decision Making in Two Cultures", Advances in Consumer Research Vol. XIV, pp. 303-308.

William Baker, J. Wesley Hutchinoson, Danny Moore, Prakash Nedungadi, (1986), "Brand Familiarity and Advertising Effects on the Evoked set and Brand Preference", Advances in Consumer Research, Richard J. Lutz edn.

William F. Massey, (1965), "On the Methods: Discriminant Analysis of Audience Characteristics", *Journal of Advertising Research,* March (5), pp. 39-48.

William O.Bearden, Rendall L.Rose, (1990), "Attention to Social Comparison Information : An Individual Difference Factor Affecting Consumer Conformity", *Journal of Consumer Research,* March, Vol. 16, 1990, pp. 461-471.

William O. Bearden, Richard G. Netemeyer & Jesse E.Teel, (1989), "Measurement of Consumer Susceptibility to Interpersonal Influence", *Journal of Consumers Research,* March, Vol. 15, pp. 473-481.

William R.Dillin, Donald G.Frederick & Vanchi Tangpanichdee, (1985), "Decision Issues in Building Perceptual Product Spaces with Multi–Attribute Rating Data", *Journal of Consumer Research,* June, Vol.12, pp. 47-53.

Woodside. Arch G, (1975), "Effects of prior Decision-Making, Demographics, and Psychographics on Martial Roles for purchasing Durables", Advances in Consumer Research, Vol.2. pp. 81-92.

Wood D., (1972), "Consumer Durables: Differentiation Strategy and Consumer Response in Relation to Real and Apparent Risk", European *Journal of Marketing,* Vol. 6, No 4.

Wright, Peter, (1975) , "Consumer Choice Strategies : Simplifying Vs. Optimising", *Journal of Marketing of Research,* (February).

Yehushua Tsal, (1985), "On the Relationship Between Cognitive and Affective Processes: A Critique of Zajonc & Markus", *Journal of Consumer Research,* Vol. 12, December , pp. 258-362.

Zarrel Y. Lambert, (1972), "Price and Choice Behaviour", *Journal of Marketing Research,* February, Vol. IX, pp. 35-40.

——, (1979), the Ranks of the Rich Get Richer, Time (July 9), p.40.

——, (1991), The Rise of the Urban consumer, The Hindu (November 7), p.17.

——, (1992), Worst Phase of Recession Over? , The Hindu Research Bureau, The Hindu, (August 24), p. 13.

——, (1967), Family Decision Making, Research Report, Time Magazine.

——, (1981), Hard Times for the Status – Minded, Time (December 21), p. 38.